The FBI
Confidential Source
Failure

The FBI Confidential Source Failure

Audit of the Federal Bureau of Investigation's
Management of its Confidential Human Source
Validation Processes

Michael Horowitz
Office of the Inspector General
U.S. Department of Justice

Thirteen Colony Press

©2019 Thirteen Colony Press

The publication of this report in no way implies any type of relationship between Thirteen Colony Press or Sastrugi Press LLC and the United States Government, the U.S. Department of State, Hillary Clinton, or any other employees or contractors therein. This book is published under Section 105 of the Copyright Act.

Thirteen Colony Press
c/o Sastrugi Press LLC
PO Box 1297, Jackson, WY 83001, United States
www.sastrugipress.com

CIP data available
U.S. Department of State
The FBI Confidential Source Failure / Michael Horowitz, Office of the Inspector General, U.S. Department of State —1st United States edition
p. cm.
1. Civics 2. Politics 3. Government
The OIG's report on the FBI's failure to comply with Attorney General Guidelines for informants relating to the 2016 FISA abuse report of the Russia dossier against presidential candidate Donald Trump.

Thirteen Colony Press is an imprint of Sastrugi Press LLC.

Printed in the United States of America when bought in the United States of America.
10 9 8 7 6 5 4 3 2 1

Sastrugi Press
00206

Table of Contents

Introduction by Michael Horowitz, Inspector General for the U.S. Department of Justice Video Transcript

Hello, I'm Michael Horowitz, Inspector General for the U.S. Department of Justice.

Today we released a report on the FBI's management of its Confidential Human Source program. The FBI relies on confidential sources to provide support for law enforcement and national security operations. But lessons learned from past confidential source problems has led Attorneys General to place a strong emphasis on oversight over confidential sources; and to the creation of the Attorney General confidential source guidelines.

We identified significant issues in our audit regarding both the FBI's oversight of its confidential sources and the FBI's compliance with the Attorney General Guidelines.

- First, we found that the FBIs' vetting processes for sources, known as validation, did not comply with the Attorney General Guidelines, particularly with regard to "long- term" sources,
- Second, we found that the Department's review committee that approves the FBI's continued use of long-term confidential sources had not vetted long-term sources in a timely manner and also did not comply with the Attorney General Guidelines.
- Third, we found that the FBI didn't provide agents with clear guidance for how to communicate with confidential sources.
- Finally, we found that FBI employees were **sometimes discouraged from documenting conclusions and recommendations about sources**; and we identified issues with the FBI's ability to align its confidential sources with its highest threat priorities.

Ineffective management and oversight of confidential sources can result in jeopardizing FBI operations, and placing FBI agents, sources, subjects of investigation, and the public in harm's way. The

FBI agreed with all of our recommendations to improve its management and oversight over this important program.

To read the report and all of our findings, visit our website, oig.justice.gov, or go to oversight.gov.

Thank you for joining us.

DOJ Press Release

DOJ OIG Releases Report on the FBI's Management of its Confidential Human Source Validation Processes

Department of Justice (DOJ) Inspector General Michael E. Horowitz announced today the release of a report examining the Federal Bureau of Investigation's (FBI) confidential human source (CHS) validation processes. The FBI's CHS validation processes involve vetting the credibility of a CHS and assessing the veracity of the information the source provides. Validation is critical to the overall integrity and reliability of the FBI's CHS program.

The DOJ Office of the Inspector General (OIG) identified numerous issues related to the FBI's validation processes. The report also discusses issues with FBI CHS communications and the FBI's ability to ensure that its CHS network aligns with the most significant identified threats. Some of the specific findings in the report released today include:

- **The FBI Did Not Comply with the AG Guidelines and Faces Ongoing Challenges in Overseeing Long-Term CHSs.** We identified a backlog of long-term CHSs awaiting required validations. Both the Attorney General Guidelines Regarding the Use of FBI CHSs (AG Guidelines) and FBI policy categorize CHSs based on several risk factors. The AG Guidelines identify "long-term" operation of a CHS – a period of greater than 5 years – as a risk factor, indicating a heightened need for validation. However, we found that the FBI did not comply with the AG Guidelines' requirements and its own policies and procedures for managing long-term CHSs by not validating all long-term CHSs after 5 years as required. By not timely reviewing long-term CHSs for continued use, the FBI risks retaining active CHSs who should have been closed for cause. We also found the FBI's long-term CHS validation reports insufficient because they did not review the full scope of a long-term

CHS's work for the FBI. Moreover, FBI employees conducting CHS validation reviews told us they were discouraged from documenting conclusions and recommendations arising from the validation process.

- **FBI's Current Validation Process Lacks Adequate Controls.** We found that the FBI has not implemented adequate controls in its latest validation process, creating a risk that CHSs are not adequately scrutinized or prioritized. Specifically, the FBI's current validation process does not provide sufficient independent FBI headquarters oversight and monitoring to ensure CHS risk is effectively mitigated.

- **Securing and Safeguarding Communications with CHSs.** We found that the FBI lacked clear guidance to inform its personnel of the acceptable platforms for communicating with CHSs. Without clear guidance, we believe there is increased operational risk that could result in agents and CHSs being put in harm's way.

- **Coverage Gaps in the FBI's Network of CHSs.** We identified issues related to the FBI's ability to align its CHSs with its highest threat priorities. Specifically, we found that the FBI lacked an automated process to analyze the threat areas in which it has CHS coverage, and relied on an ineffective process that could result in outdated information. In addition, we found that a proposed automated system being developed would rely on data from several other FBI systems, including its CHS system of record which has known issues related to data quality.

Today's report makes 16 recommendations to assist the FBI and the Department of Justice in improving the FBI's CHS program. The FBI and Department of Justice agreed with all 16 recommendations and has started corrective measures.

The OIG initiated this audit in 2018, and had previously conducted reviews of the human source programs at the Bureau of Alcohol, Tobacco, Firearms and Explosives (ATF) in 2017 and the Drug

Enforcement Agency (DEA) in 2016 and 2015.

Report: Today's report is available on the OIG's website under "Recent Reports" and at the following link: https://oig.justice.gov/reports/2019/a20009.pdf.

Video: To accompany today's report, the OIG has released a 2-minute video featuring the Inspector General discussing the report's findings. The video and a downloadable transcript are available at the following link: https://oig.justice.gov/multimedia/video-11-19-19.htm.

Executive Summary

Audit of the Federal Bureau of Investigation's Management of its Confidential Human Source Validation Processes

(U) Objectives

(U) The objectives of this audit were to: (1) evaluate the Federal Bureau of Investigation's (FBI) Confidential Human Source (CHS) program policies and procedures, including its validation procedures; (2) assess the FBI's policies and procedures for the use of non-attributable communications between agents and CHSs; and (3) examine the FBI's ability to identify and fill gaps in the alignment of its CHSs with the nation's highest priority threats and intelligence needs.

(U) Results in Brief

(U) We found that the FBI's vetting process for CHSs, known as validation, did not comply with the Attorney General Guidelines. We also found deficiencies in the FBI's long-term CHS validation reports which are relied upon by FBI and Department of Justice (Department or DOJ) officials in determining the continued use of a CHS. Further, the FBI inadequately staffed and trained personnel conducting long-term validations and lacked an automated process to monitor its long-term CHSs.

(U) The joint DOJ-FBI committee tasked with oversight of the FBI's CHS program did not meet its composition requirements placing an undue burden on just a few members. Thecommitteealso had a backlog of CHSs awaiting continued use determinations, potentially allowing them to operate when they should not have.

(U) The FBI also missed an opportunity to identify its non-compliance with established CHS validation requirements because it did not follow its own directives for incorporating new procedures into policy. Further, we identified issues related to the FBI's current validation process for CHSs with characteristics the FBI considers significant and its lack of policy for communicatingwithCHSs. Lastly, a newly proposed system designed to align its CHS base with its highest priorities will rely on ingesting data from at least one FBI system with known data quality issues.

(U) Recommendations

(U) Our report contains 16 recommendations to help the FBI better manage its CHS program.

(U) Audit Results

(U) Between FY 2012 and FY 2018 the FBI spent an average of $42 million annually in payments to its CHSs. As of May 2019, nearly 20 percent of the FBI's CHS base met its definition of a long-term CHS. As we conducted our audit, of particular concern was the FBI's management of these long-term CHSs.

(U) FBI Did Not Comply with the AG Guidelines and Faces Ongoing Challenges in Overseeing Long-Term CHSs - The FBI uses CHSs to provide intelligence and support law enforcement and national security operations. The Attorney General Guidelines Regarding the Use of FBI Confidential Human Sources (AG Guidelines) and the FBI categorize CHSs based on several risk factors.

(U) We found that the FBI did not comply with the AG Guidelines' requirements and its own policies and procedures for managing long-term CHSs and, consequently, a backlog of CHSs awaited validation. In addition, the FBI's long-term CHS validation reports were insufficient because they did not ensure the full scope of a long-term CHS's operation was reviewed and FBI validation personnel told us they were discouraged from documenting conclusions and recommendations. Further, the number of personnel tasked with conducting long-term CHS validations was insufficient due to the size of the long-term CHS validation backlog and the lack of adequate training. The FBI also lacked an automated process to identify, track, and monitor long-term CHSs, and there was no automated process to document approvals that allow the same agent to continue to manage a CHS in excess of five years.

(U) These factors increase the likelihood that the FBI has not adequately mitigated the risks associated with long term CHSs, including the risks posed by overly familiar and non-objective handling agent and CHS relationships.

(U) FBI officials told us that they did not believe "long term" to be a useful indicator in determining CHS risk and, towards the conclusion of our audit work, the FBI indicated that it now intends to pursue discussions with DOJ on the AG Guidelines long-term CHS validation requirements.

(U) Human Source Review Committee Was Not Composed According to Requirements and Faces an Ongoing Backlog - The joint DOJ and FBI Human Source Review Committee (HSRC) did not comply with the composition requirements set forth in the AG Guidelines and a backlog of CHSs awaited the HSRC's continued use determinations. By not meeting the composition requirement for the HSRC, an undue burden was placed on a few HSRC members to keep up with the workload.

(U) Further, by not reviewing these long-term CHSs for continued use in a timely manner, some CHSs may have remained active when they should have been closed or had additional conditions placed on their continued use. For example, we found that the HSRC requested a CHS be closed because the CHS was a child sex offender and the HSRC did not believe the benefits of using the CHS outweighed the associated risks. Because of the current backlog of long-term CHSs awaiting validations at the FBI, important continued use determinations like this may not occur for significant periods of time.

(U) FBI Did Not Follow Its Policy Implementation Process When Revising Validation Practices - Between 2011 and 2019, the Directorate of Intelligence (DI) implemented different validation processes without incorporating them into policy. Instead, various electronic communications were issued to provide guidance on the revised processes. Because the DI did not incorporate the revised validation processes into policy, it missed the opportunity to go through the formal deconfliction process that should have identified its non-compliance with AG Guidelines requirements for long-term CHSs. To date, the most recent iteration of the validation process, developed in 2017, has not been incorporated as policy.

(U) FBI's Current Validation Process Lacks Adequate Independent Oversight and Should Be Reengineered - We found that the FBI has not implemented adequate controls in its latest validation process, creating a risk that CHSs are not adequately scrutinized or prioritized. The FBI's current validation process does not provide sufficient independent FBI headquarters oversight and monitoring to ensure CHS risk is effectively mitigated.

(U) FBI's Annual CHS Validation Report and the Communication of its Importance Should be Improved - While we found that the FBI's annual CHS validation report met the minimum requirement of the AG Guidelines, we determined that the report may not be sufficiently addressing CHS risk. In addition, we found that the importance of the annual CHS report in the overall validation process has not been adequately communicated to FBI field offices.

(U) Challenges Exist in Securing and Safeguarding CHS Communications and Information - We found that the FBI lacked clear guidance to inform its personnel of the acceptable platforms for communicating with CHSs. For example, we found varying practices and opinions among FBI field offices on whether government-issued cell phones were an acceptable method to communicate with a CHS. Without clear guidance, we believe there is increased operational security risk that could result in agents and CHSs being put in harm's way. In addition, we found that the FBI is not ensuring its highly classified CHS reporting platform is properly safeguarded from unauthorized access, increasing the potential for unmitigated insider threat risks.

(U) FBI Should Prioritize Automation of its Processes to Identify and Fill Gaps in CHS Coverage - We identified issues related to the FBI's ability to align its CHSs with its highest threat priorities. Specifically, we found that the FBI lacked an automated process to analyze its CHS coverage and relied on an ineffective process that was time consuming and resulted in potentially outdated information. Although we learned that the FBI was developing a system to automate its assessment of CHS placement to address these deficiencies, we determined that the proposed system would rely on data from several other FBI systems, including its CHS system of record, which has known issues related to data quality.

INTRODUCTION

(U) Confidential Human Sources (CHS) play a critical role in the Federal Bureau of Investigation's (FBI) operations. The Attorney General's Guidelines Regarding the Use of FBI Confidential Human Sources (AG Guidelines) define a CHS as any individual who is believed to be providing useful and credible information to the FBI and whose identity, information, or relationship with the FBI warrants confidential handling. Because of the important role of CHSs, vetting the credibility of CHSs and assessing the veracity of the information they provide is critical to the overall integrity and reliability of the FBI's CHS program. This process, known as validation, is a fundamental responsibility of intelligence collectors, including the FBI. Validation serves as an essential component of FBI human intelligence (HUMINT) because it assists in ensuring that information obtained from any CHS is accurate, authentic, reliable, and free from undisclosed influence.

(U) The U.S. intelligence and law enforcement communities place a strong emphasis on CHS validation because of lessons learned from various historical operations. For example, it was the FBI's mishandling of informant James "Whitey" Bulger, a long-term CHS for the FBI who was tipped off by his FBI handling agent and fled prosecution but was later arrested that spurred, in large part, a review of the AG Guidelines.[41] These operations demonstrated the importance of ensuring independent and objective FBI headquarters oversight of the relationship between handling agents and CHSs in order to avoid the pitfalls associated with poor operational security and overly familiar relationships.

(S//NF) In addition to properly vetting CHSs, communicating and documenting contacts with CHSs are important aspects of the FBI's intelligence gathering process. Further, it is vital for the FBI to have a sufficient CHS base that is aligned with its highest priorities

---

41 The multiple FBI management and oversight failures of Bulger's time as a CHS, including Bulger's crimes such as murder and racketeering while being handled as an FBI CHS, are documented in a case study in the OIG's report *The Federal Bureau of Investigation's Compliance with the Attorney General's Investigative Guidelines* (September 2005).

and the greatest threats to the American people. For example, it is important to have CHSs embedded in terrorist cells, violent gangs, and espionage operations, among others, in order to collect valuable intelligence and investigative information. As of May 2019, the FBI managed [REDACTED] active CHSs, including [REDACTED] long-term CHSs whom the FBI had registered as CHSs for more than 5 consecutive years.[42] The FBI spent an average of $42 million annually in payments to CHSs from FY 2012 through FY 2018.

(U) FBI CHS Guidance and Policy

The AG Guidelines govern the use of FBI CHSs. As a result of lessons learned, the guidelines were most recently revised in December 2006, including the creation of special provisions for long-term CHSs and a Human Source Review Committee (HSRC) to approve a long-term CHS's continued use.[43] The AG Guidelines apply to the use of CHSs in both criminal and national security investigations, although certain oversight requirements differ depending on whether the CHS is reporting on criminal or national security matters. The AG Guidelines also require validation activities at various intervals, including initial and annual CHS validations, and enhanced validations for certain special categories of CHSs, such as long-term CHSs.[44]

(U) In addition to the AG Guidelines, the U.S. Intelligence Community provides CHS validation guidance through its National HUMINT Manager Directive 001.08, which establishes a common set of validation standards for collectors of intelligence.[45] To provide guidance to its workforce on the implementation of the AG Guidelines and the U.S. Intelligence Community validation standards, the FBI issued a CHS Policy Guide (Policy Guide) and a CHS Validation Standards Manual (Validation Manual). The Policy Guide was

---

42 The AG Guidelines use this criteria to define long-term.

43 The AG Guidelines specify that certain Department and FBI officials are required to participate in the HSRC.

44 The AG Guidelines define special categories of CHSs as those that are: (1) senior leadership CHSs, (2) privileged or media CHSs, (3) high-level government or union CHSs; and (4) long-term CHSs.

45 The Director of the Central Intelligence Agency serves as the National HUMINT Manager. The National HUMINT Manager Directive 001.08 became effective January 18, 2008.

established to ensure consistent application of CHS program policies in all FBI investigative programs and to promote compliance with the AG Guidelines.[46] The purpose of the Validation Manual is to standardize CHS validation procedures across investigative programs.[47]

(U) CHS Program Management

(U) The FBI's Directorate of Intelligence (DI) is responsible for the development and oversight of the FBI's CHS program, including the implementation of the Policy Guide and the Validation Manual. Within the DI, the HUMINT Operations Section, among its other responsibilities, is responsible for ensuring that the FBI's policies are consistent with the AG Guidelines. In addition, the HUMINT Operations Section is responsible for providing guidance to all field offices, legal attaches, and FBI Headquarters' divisions to ensure their respective CHSs are in compliance with FBI, DOJ, and U.S. Intelligence Community directives. Further, the HUMINT Operations Section is responsible for ensuring CHSs with the highest risk potential are vetted according to established policies and procedures.

(U) Within the HUMINT Operations Section, there are multiple units, including the HUMINT Services Unit II and the Validation Management Unit (Validation Unit). The HUMINT Services Unit II's responsibilities include CHS policy revisions, and it serves as the program management unit for all CHS policy matters as they relate to CHSoperations. The Validation Unit's responsibilities include program management and oversight responsibilities for CHSs through the FBI's validation process.

(U) At the field offices, the Assistant Director in Charge or Special Agent in Charge (SAC) is responsible for ensuring a local CHS program that contributes to the FBI's collective CHS base.[48] To

---

46 The FBI released its first CHS Policy Manual in 2007. The 2007 CHS Policy Manual was superseded by the Policy Guide in March 2012 and it was most recently revised in October 2016.

47 The FBI's first released its CHS Validation Manual in August 2007 and it was last updated in March 2010.

48 Based on the size of the offices, the FBI has Assistant Directors in Charge in 3 of its 56 field offices. The remaining 53 field offices are headed by SACs.

assist in fulfilling this responsibility, Special Agents in the field offices ("handling agents") recruit, vet, handle, and communicate with CHSs. In addition, supervisors oversee handling agents and are responsible for the completion of quarterly CHS reporting. FBI Assistant Special Agents in Charge (ASAC) are responsible for reviewing and submitting annual CHS reports, that serve as the field office's review of the CHS file - a responsibility that cannotbedelegated. ToassistinCHScomplianceandoversightrequirements,the Policy Guide requires that each field office must have at least one CHS Coordinator who acts as a liaison with FBI headquarters and other field offices regarding CHS matters.

(U) FBI Validation Processes

(U) The AG Guidelines set forth certain CHS validation requirements, including annual and long-term CHS validations, and the FBI incorporated processes in its Validation Manual to meet these requirements. In addition, the FBI implemented various validation processes based on additional CHS risk factors it identified. TheFBI'svalidationprocesses,boththoserequiredbytheAGGuidelines and those that it has implemented as a result of CHS risk factors the FBI believes to be higher risk, have changed over time. For example, all CHSs must receive an annual CHS review but the oversight of the review has shifted from FBI headquarterstothefieldoffices. AsdiscussedintheAuditResultssectionofthis report, in 2013 the FBI implemented a new validation process, which deviated from its long-term CHS validation process as described in its Validation Manual and failed to prioritize long-term CHSs. Consequently, in fiscal year 2016 the FBI discovered thatithadabacklogoflong-termCHSsawaitingvalidations. Inresponse,theFBI developed a new, separate validation process for long-term CHSs. We discuss these processes further in the *Audit Results*.

(U) Audit Approach

(U) The objectives of this audit were to: (1) evaluate the FBI's CHS program policies and procedures, including its validation procedures; (2) assess the FBI's policies and practices for the use of non-attributable communications between agents and CHSs; and (3) examine the FBI's ability to identify and fill gaps in the alignment of its CHSs with the nation's highest priority threats and intelligence needs. Toaccomplishourauditobjectives,weinterviewedFBIheadquarters officials, as well as officials at FBI field offices in Philadelphia, Pennsylvania and Washington, D.C. In addition, we interviewed Department officials and officials from another intelligence agency to gain an understanding of how its programs function. Wealso(1)reviewedtheAGGuidelines,theNationalHUMINTManager Directive 001.08, and FBI CHS policies and procedures; (2) analyzed CHS-related data; and (3) examined documents relating to CHS management, oversight, and validation. This audit primarily covers the FBI's CHS program from fiscal year (FY) 2012 through May 2019.

(U) The results of our review are detailed in the Audit Results section of this report. Our audit objectives, scope, and methodology are discussed in further detail in Appendix 1. We also reviewed prior reports conducted by the OIG and FBI related to the management and oversight of CHSs. Details of these reports can be found in Appendix 2.

(U) AUDIT RESULTS

(U) We found significant weaknesses with certain aspects of the FBI's CHS program. First, regarding long-term CHSs, we found that the FBI failed to comply with AG Guidelines' validation requirements and its own validation policies and procedures. Related to this finding, we also identified issues with the FBI's long term CHS validation reports, which serve an important function when determinationsaremadeonthecontinueduseofalong-termCHS. In addition, insufficient resources and inadequately trained personnel who conducted long-term validations increased the likelihood that some of the risks associated with long-term CHSs were not mitigated. We also found that the FBI lacked an automated process to identify, track, and monitor its long-term CHSs or to document continued agent handling approvals in FBI field offices. Second, we found that the joint DOJ and FBI Human Source Review Committee (HSRC) consistently fell short of the composition requirements of the AG Guidelines and operated with a backlog of long-term CHSs awaiting continuing use determinations. Third, we found that because the FBI changed its process for validating CHSs without following its own directives for incorporating new processes and procedures into policy, it missed an opportunity to go through the formal deconfliction process that should have identified its non compliance with AG Guidelines requirements for long-term CHSs. Fourth, we determined that the FBI's current validation process for CHSs with characteristics the FBI considers significant lacks sufficient independent headquarters oversight and monitoring to ensure CHS risk is effectively mitigated. Fifth, we found that the FBI's annual CHS validation report may not be sufficiently addressing CHS risk. Sixth, we identified areas that can be improved related to CHS communications. Finally, we found that the FBI was in the process of developing a system to align its CHSs with its highest threat priorities. However, we determined that the proposed system relies on utilizing data from several other FBI systems, including its Delta system, which has known data quality issues.[49]

---

49 (U) Delta is the FBI's official electronic record-keeping system for CHS management. According

(U) FBI Did Not Comply with the AG Guidelines and Faces On-going Challenges in Overseeing Long-Term CHSs

(U) The FBI uses CHSs in all types of investigations, as they can provide ongoing intelligence to support law enforcement and national security operations. The AG Guidelines and the FBI categorize CHSs based on a number of factors, such as their placement or access within certain organizations and the length of time serving as a CHS, which was of particular concern to us as we conducted our audit. According to the AG Guidelines and FBI policy, a long-term CHS is defined as one thathasbeenregisteredformorethanfive-consecutiveyears. Asweconducted our audit, of particular concern was the FBI's management of long-term CHSs.

(U) *FBI Did Not Adhere to Long-Term CHS Validation Requirements and Should Ensure Policies and Procedures Comply with the AG Guidelines*

(SI/NF) The AG Guidelines and the FBI's Validation Manual require that all special category CHSs, such as long-term CHSs, receive an enhanced review every 5 years. According to the Validation Manual, an enhanced review includes (1) [REDACTED]; (2) a production review; and (3) [REDACTED].[50] However, we found that the FBI did not ensure that all long-term CHSs received an enhanced review every 5 years and repeatedly deviated from its Validation Manual guidance for enhanced validations, which contributed to a backlog of long-term CHSs awaiting validations. This backlog, originally identified by the FBI in 2015, has continued to persist and, according to the FBI, [REDACTED] long-term CHSs (or nearly half of FBI's long-term CHS base) awaited validation as of May 2019.[51] We believe that several factors contributed to the FBI's non-compliance with the AG Guidelines and its Validation Manual, including the 2011 development of a new validation prioritization system, insufficient headquarters validation resources, and frequent

to the FBI, Delta was intended to facilitate compliance with the AG Guidelines and FBI CHS policies through automated administrative and management functions.

50 (U) Production reviews seek to identify all CHS reporting and verify the reporting.

51 (U) The FBI provided this data to the OIG but we were not able to verify the number due to Delta's limitation in accurately identifying long-term CHSs requiring validations. We discuss these limitations later in this report.

leadership turnover in the Directorate of Intelligence.

(U) Implementation of a New Validation Prioritization System

(U) In 2011, the DI began developing a new validation process to identify and prioritize CHSs with certain risk factors. This process, known as the CHS Prioritization System (CPS), sought to direct headquarters validation resources to its riskiest CHSs. FBI headquarters' validation units began using CPS in January 2013 and CPS was implemented for use in Delta by all field offices in September 2013.[52]

(S I/■ N F) According to FBI documentation, the initial CPS was based on a series of [REDACTED] value-weighted, cross-programatic risk factors that were used to rank all CHSs by potential risk profiles. Each category was assigned a number between 2 and 5 corresponding to the risk, with 2 being the lowest risk and 5 being the highest risk. All applicable risk categories were then totaled and prioritized into three tiers, with a focus on Tier 1 validations first. Long-term CHSs were given a risk number of 3 for the "long-term" risk factor. We determined that, under this scoring system, it was possible to be a long-term CHS and not be prioritized for validation, because CHSs whose only risk factor was that they were long-term would fail to score as a Tier 1 CHS in any programmatic area. In December 2015, the FBI revised its CPS risk categories and its methodology for prompting a validation. Under the revised CPS, the FBI eliminated "long-term" as a risk factor altogether, making it even less likely that a long-term CHS would be prioritized for validation. We recognize the FBI's efforts to prioritize its limited validation resources to what it believes to be its riskiest CHSs through the development of CPS. As part of that effort, DI management may have determined, despite prior instances of serious misconduct by long term CHSs, that the evidence no longer supports including

---

52 (U) At the time the Validation Manual was issued in March 2010, FBI headquarters had multiple validation units based on program areas. While the March 2010 Validation Manual was the primary CHS validation guidance at the time of our audit, FBI headquarters no longer had multiple validation units. The Validation Unit is the only validation unit that existed within the HUMINT Operations Section during this audit.

"long term" as a risk factor. However, we are concerned that, rather than elevating to senior Department leadership its concern with the AG Guidelines' requirement that all long-term CHSs receive an enhanced review every five years, DI management on its own decided to implement a new review system that does not comply with the AG Guidelines.[53]

(U) FBI officials from the Directorate of Intelligence told us that they did not believe "long-term" to be a useful indicator in determining CHS risk, that long-term validations are not a priority for the FBI, and, towards the conclusion of our audit work, that it now intends to pursue discussions with the Department to modify the AG Guidelines long-term CHS validation requirements. However, we identified instances of management and oversight failures involving long-term CHSs. For example, an August 2017 FBI Office of Professional Responsibility investigation determined that a field office handling agent had an improper relationship with CHSs that included entertaining at least one long-term CHS at the handling agent's personal residence on multiple occasions. An FBI headquarters official who was tasked with assisting that same handling agent stated that he "had never experienced such poor operational security when it came to the handling and briefing of CHSs."

(U) Given these past instances of misconduct involving long term CHSs, absent strong evidence that long term CHSs are no longer a risk, we believe long term should be included as a factor in assessing CHS risk to ensure the pitfalls that may occur with long-term CHSs, including overly familiar relationships and poor operational security, are avoided. We recommend the FBI ensures that the DI designs, implements, and adheres to validation policies and procedures for its long term CHSs that comply with the AG Guidelines, or coordinate with the Department to seek revisions to the AG Guidelines, as necessary.

---

53 (U) As discussed later in this report, the FBI developed in 2017 the Significant Source Review Panel as a process for identifying what it believes to be the most significant CHSs for validation. This new process was separate from both the CPS and its long-term CHS validation process. Although the FBI still utilizes all three of these processes, the FBI told us that it now dedicates most of its resources and efforts to the Significant Source Review Panel for identifying CHSs for validation.

(U) Insufficient Validation Resources

(U) We believe that a reduction in the number of Intelligence Analysts conducting validations also contributed to the FBI's non-compliance with long-term CHS requirements. From the issuance of its   10 Validation Manual through the time of our audit, FBI leadership has significantly reduced the number of intelligence analysts conducting validations at headquarters. In February 2010, the FBI had 213 FBI headquarters personnel dedicated to validation efforts. As of March 2019, FBI headquarters had only a single validation unit comprised of 29 personnel - an 86 percent decrease in FBI headquarters validation personnel since February 2010.

(U) When we asked why such a significant decrease occurred, the FBI Assistant Director for the Resource Planning Office told us that in anticipation of the 2013 sequestration spending cuts, the FBI identified certain FBI headquarters resources to be cut, including a portion of Di's Intelligence Analysts. The same official explained that when sequestration did not come to pass as expected, the resources were not restored and were instead re-allocated to the field offices.

(U//FOUO) At the time the DI initially discovered the backlog in 2015, it did not have sufficient validation resources and proposed that the Inspection Division conduct a Special Inspection using Assistant Inspectors-in-Place to help reduce the long-term CHS backlog.[54] The FBI told us that this Special Inspection employed 33 Assistant Inspectors-in-Place to conduct validations at FBI headquarters over a 10- day period beginning February 2016. We asked the FBI to provide us with documentation that demonstrated the success of the Special Inspection in reducing the backlog. However, the evidence provided to us was insufficient and we could not confirm the results of the effort. Further, the FBI did not provide any documentation demonstrating an increase in validation personnel to ensure compliance with the AG Guidelines long-term CHS

---

54 (U) FBI personnel must be either a Supervisory Special Agent (SSA) or a Supervisory Intelligence Analyst to be eligible to participate as an Assistant Inspector-in-Place. According to the FBI, Assistant Inspectors-in-Place may be canvassed by the FBI Inspection Division to participate in National Program Reviews and Field Office, Legal Attache, and Special Inspections.

validation requirements. Therefore, even if the Special Inspection temporarily mitigated the extent of backlog, the FBI did not allocate sufficient resources after the Special Inspection to ensure compliance with the AG Guidelines requirements for long-term CHSs and prevent the FBI's admitted backlog of [REDACTED] long-term CHS's awaiting validation as of May 2019.

(S//NF) The FBI's Inspection Division identified an issue related to validation resources in a 2013 National Program Review (2013 National Program Review) of its CHS program and recommended the DI "analyze the effect of any reduction in staffing on the number and quality of validations." However, we were unable to obtain documentation that the DI attempted to remedy this recommendation, in part, because the Inspection Division's resolution process did not require the DI to demonstrate that the recommendation had been implemented. Given an active CHS base of [REDACTED] CHSs as of May 2019, including [REDACTED] long-term CHSs, we do not believe the DI has taken appropriate corrective actions to ensure sufficient validation personnel are allocated to fulfill the long-term CHS oversight function in compliance with the AG Guidelines.

(U) Because it did not allocate sufficient resources to validate all long-term CHSs in accordance with the AG Guidelines, the FBI increased its risk of missing warning signs, especially for questionable CHSs. We recommend that the FBI dedicate sufficient resources to ensure that long-term CHS validations, including backlogged long-term CHS validations, are conducted in accordance with the requirements of the AG Guidelines.

(U) DI Leadership Turnover

(U) We believe leadership turnover within the DI may have also contributed to the FBI's non-compliance with long-term CHS requirements because executives didnotremaininpositionslongenoughtocompletecertaininitiatives. Inthe2013 National Program Review, the FBI's Inspection Division noted that an updated Validation Manual was "pending final approval." The same review determined that failing to make timely updates and revisions to policy had created policy gaps and widespreadconfusion. Durin-gouraudit,wefoundthattheFBIneverapprovedan updated Validation Manual, and one FBI official told us that it was never finalized due to leadership turnover within the DI. Another FBI official also stated that because the DI has experienced ongoing turnover of executive management, the DI continues to have challenges for-malizing policy. Additionally, we found that most FBI officials with contemporaneous knowledge of CHS validation non-compliance issues, such as long-term CHS validations and the related backlog, were no longer assigned to the DI and several officials rotated to field office positions during our audit. We also found that many DI units were headed by FBI officials in an acting capacity, which may make it more difficult for policy and resource improvements to be implemented.

(U) *Long-Term CHS Validation Report Needs Improvement*

(U) In late 2015, the DI created a new long-term CHS validation report intended to be a streamlined product that would effectively and efficiently address the long-term CHS backlog and provide the standard for future long-term CHS validations. We reviewed the long-term CHS validation report and its related guidance and found that it failed to sufficiently account for the full scope of a CHS's use, regardless of whether the CHS had operated for 5 years, 10 years, or longer. While we determined that the long-term CHS validation report required validation personnel to review the last 5 years of a CHSs' field office annual reports, as we discuss later in this report, we found the annual reports may not adequately address CHS risk.

(U) In addition, we found that the long-term CHS validation report was limited to: (1) 1 year of in-depth file review; (2) certain CHS database checks; and (3) CHS production reviews, which an-alyze a CHS's contributions, but do not include the corroboration of information.[55] Aside from these issues with the scope of the

---

55 (S//NF) According to the FBI's Validation Manual, a CHS production review addresses a CHSs productivity in detail. [REDACTED]
(S//NF) [REDACTED]

long-term CHS validation report, we also identified issues with the related guidance because it discouraged validation personnel from making any overall conclusions or recommendations based on the information gathered.[56]

(U) We discussed the long-term CHS validation report with a Department official who participates on the HSRC and relies on the information to approve the continued use of long-term CHSs. The Department official told us that HSRC members lacked insight into the FBI's long-term CHS validation-process, and expressed concerns that database checks only examined 1 or 2 years, rather than the full 5-year period or longer. Further, this official told us that it is important for FBI headquarters validation personnel to have the ability to draw conclusions and make recommendations as those conclusions and recommendations are valuable to the HSRC members.

> (U) HSRC MEMBER QUOTES
>
> **(U) "... deeply concerned that the limited scope of the long-term validation review may potentially be omitting important information and critical red flags that the HSRC members rely on to approve the ongoing use of long-term CHSs."**
> **(U) "The limited scope of information in the [validation] reports places those individuals deciding the continued use of long-term CHSs in a terrible decision-making position."**

(U) We believe that because the long-term CHS validation report did not ensure that the entire scope of a long-term CHS's operation is reviewed and reported, it may have increased the likelihood that red flags or anomalies were omitted. Inaddition,theabsenceofconclusionsorrecommendationsmayhave deprived HSRC members of sufficient information to make continued use decisions. We recommend that the FBI coordinate with the Department and update, as necessary, its long-term CHS validation report to ensure that it addresses the appropriate scope of review and memorializes any validation personnel's conclusions or recommendations.

---

56 (U) Conclusions and recommendations can include such examples as continuing to operate the CHS, polygraphing a CHS, or engaging in operational testing of the CHS.

(U) *FBI Did Not Ensure Appropriate Staffing To Conduct Long-Term CHS Validations and Will Continue to Face Challenges Without Adequate Resources*

(U) An FBI official told us that in 2017 the responsibility for conducting long term CHS validations was moved from the Validation Unit to the HUMINT Services Unit II. This change was made so that the Validation Unit could focus on other types of validation reports. However, we found that the HUMINT Services Unit II did not have a cadre of trained intelligence analysts to perform long-term validations. For example, the only HUMINT Services Unit II Supervisory Special Agent (SSA) tasked with conducting long-term CHS validations from July 2017 through August 2018 told us that she did not receive adequate training to write intelligence products. In fact, she told us that she only received on-the-job training, whereas, intelligence analysts typically receive 13 weeks of formal training, including multiple weeks of analytical writing courses. A second SSA who was brought in to replace the first SSA when she returned to the field in January 2019 told us that he did not have the background or skills to be conducting validations and was not aware that he would be conducting them when he took the position. He added that he was doing nothing more than he would have done as a field supervisor because he was reviewing annual CHS reports solely for completeness and was not doing any "deep diving" in the CHS files.

(U) This same individual also told us that he received his training from the SSA who herself had advised us that she did not receive adequate training. By not ensuring personnel were adequately trained, those tasked with conducting long term CHS validations risked missing anomalies and red flags that could have harmed operational security.

(U) In addition to inadequately trained staff, we also found that staffing levels were not adequate to address the volume of long-term CHS validations. As noted above, from July 2017 through August 2018, only one individual was assigned to conduct long-term CHS validations. This same individual told us that clearing the backlog was an impossible task for one person and believed it would only continue to grow with the limited resources dedicated to conducting long-term CHS validations. We believe that inadequate staffing was a primary contributor to the increasing backlog.

(U//FOUO) The DI recognized these risks and, in April 2019, the Chief of the Validation Unit told us that responsibility for conducting long-term CHS validations would be returned to the Validation Unit. Nevertheless, the lack of validation resources remains a concern. According to documentation provided by the Chief of the Validation Unit, each Intelligence Analyst would be responsible for conducting two long-term CHS validations per quarter. As of March 2019, the Validation Unit had only 18 Intelligence Analysts. Accordingly, only 36 long-term CHS validations would be conducted per quarter or 144 per year. Based on this staffing level, we do not believe the Validation Unit will be able to significantly decrease the backlog of [REDACT] long-term CHSs awaiting validation. We recommend that the FBI develop a strategy to eliminate the existing backlog of long-term CHSs and perform an assessment of its current resources dedicated to long-term validations to ensure staff are appropriately trained and able to maintain their expected workload.

(U) *Lack of Reliable Process to Identify and Monitor Long-Term CHSs Hinders the FBI's Ability to Comply with the AG Guidelines*

(U) Delta is the FBI's official electronic record-keeping system for CHS management. According to the FBI, Delta was intended to facilitate compliance with the AG Guidelines and FBI CHS policies through automated administrative and managementfunctions. However, we found that Delta lacked anautomated workflow that: (1) reliably identified all long-term CHSs; (2) notified the appropriate unit that a validation was due; and (3) tracked long-term CHSs to ensureavalidationwascompleted. As a result, the FBI was unable to reliably quantify the backlog.

(U) An FBI official told us that the Delta system neither automatically updates a CHS file when a CHS meets the definitton for long-term by having been in existence for 5 consecutive years or more nor contains a workflow designed to automatically notify the unit tasked with conducting long-term validations. For the FBI to be able to provide us an estimate of its backlog, it had to manually create a spreadsheet to identify those CHSs that were long-term, and review each of those CHS's Delta files to determine if a validation had been performed in the past two years.

(U) We discussed these deficiencies with FBI officials who told us that Delta can be updated when a CHS becomes a long-term CHS, however, this only occurs if the handling agent manually enters the information. A January 2019 Delta data assessment found this process unnecessarily prone to error, particularly given that the date field could be automatically calculated.[57] According to FBI documentation, the FBI was working on Delta upgrades to both automatically update CHSs when they become long-term and to send email notifications that a validation was due at thattime. However,these upgrades had not been implemented at the time of this audit.

(U) We believe the inadequate design of Delta hindered the FBI's ability to ensure long-term CHSs were identified, tracked, and monitored. Although the FBI has considered improvements to address the shortcomings, it has not taken corrective action by implementing an automated mechanism in Delta. We recommend that the FBI develop and implement an automated mechanism in its Delta system to ensure that long-term CHSs are accurately identified and monitored, including an automated notification to the headquarters unit responsible for conducting long-term CHS validations.

(U) *Inadequate Controls Over Continued Handling of CHSs Beyond 5 Years by the Same Handling Agent Increased the Risks of Improper CHS Relationships*

(U) According to the FBI's Policy Guide, the continued handling of a long term CHS by the same handling agent for 5 consecutive

---

57 (U) A contractor was used to conduct the assessment to provide the FBI with an understanding of the data contained in Delta.

years, and every 5 consecutive years thereafter, requires SAC approval. In addition, this approval may not be delegated, and the SAC may only approve continued handling by the same handing agent for good cause. The FBI's Policy Guide definition of 'good cause' included the following justifications:

> (1) whether the handling agent has a unique role in an investigation supported by the CHS, to the extent that the investigation may face impediments due to reassignment of the handling agent; (2) whether reassignment of the handling agent would diminish the FBI's ability to obtain information in a reliable manner due to the sophisticated or technical nature of the CHS reporting and the knowledge base of the handling agent; or (3) whether there are other circumstances that affect the effective operation of the CHS, including the availability of other handling agents with the requisite experience or capability to operate the CHS.

(U) We determined that the FBI did not ensure that all handling agents requested and received SAC approval for the continued handling of CHSs in excess of5years. Whenwerequesteddocumentationofthoseapprovals,weweretold Delta does not automatically remind agents to seek approval for continued handling of a CHS beyond 5 years. In instances where the SAC approval was requested and received, the FBI did not ensure that the approval or disapproval and related justification were consistently documented.

(U) Because of Delta's limitations, the FBI could not provide us with a universe of requests for approval for continued CHS handling. However, an FBI official was able to manually create a partial spreadsheet of this data, by reviewing the files of long-term CHSs whose information had been forwarded to the HSRC for continued use approval.[58] This spreadsheet included a calendar year 2018 sample of 37 CHSs who had the same handling agents for at least

---

58 (U) As part of the HSRC process, all handling agents must answer an HSRC questionnaire. The HSRC questionnaire includes a question that asks the handling agent whether or not they have sought SAC approval for continued handling in excess of 5 years.

five-years.[59] Of those 37, a total of 8 did not include any reason justifying the continued handling by the same agent. For the remaining 29 CHSs, although we did not assess the validity, a justification was provided for approving the agents' continued handling of the CHS that was generally based on the CHS's trust of the handling agent, rapport, and productivity of the CHS. The FBI did not provide us with any evidence of disapprovals.

(U) We were informed during this audit that the FBI requested an upgrade to Delta to include an automated workflow for SAC approvals for continued handling ofCHSsbythesamehandlingagentinexcessoffiveyears. However,thisupgrade has not yet been implemented. Limiting the amount of time an agent is permitted to handle a CHS mitigates the risk of an agent compromising objectivity or developing an overly familiar relationship with a CHS. We recommend that the FBI develop and implement an automated workflow in Delta to ensure that all handling agents request and document SAC approval or disapproval for the continued handling of CHSs in excess of 5 years.

(U) Human Source Review Committee Was Not Composed According to Requirements and Faces an Ongoing Backlog

(U) After a long-term CHS has received a validation, the AG Guidelines require the FBI to seek approval for continued use of the long-term CHS from the HSRC.[60] The HSRC is comprised of both Department and FBI officials, with specific composition requirements defined by the AG Guidelines for both components. As we discuss below, the OIG identified weaknesses in both the Department's and the FBI's compliance with the AG Guidelines HSRC requirements.

(U) The Department and the FBI Did Not Comply with Human

---

59 (U) The FBI official who provided the sample told us that she was not able to provide the complete universe of continued handling requests because of limitations of Delta.

60 (U) While the AG Guidelines require all long-term CHSs to receive an enhanced validation, those CHSs providing information for use in national security investigations or foreign intelligence collections are exempt from the HSRC requirements.

Source Review Committee Composition Requirements

(U) We determined that both the Department and the FBI did not comply with AG Guidelines composition requirements for the HSRC. The AG Guidelines require that each HSRC includes a Chairperson who should be an FBI agent at or above the Deputy Assistant Director level. In addition, each HSRC shall include two FBI Agents, two attorneys from the FBI's Office of General Counsel (OGC), and five federal prosecuting office attorneys. The AG Guidelines specify that of the five federal prosecuting office attorneys, one should be a Deputy Assistant Attorney General (DAAG) from the Criminal Division and at least two shall be from U.S. Attorney's Offices and have experience in organized crime matters. In addition to the five federal prosecuting attorneys with voting power on the HSRC, the AG Guidelines require the Assistant Attorney General (AAG) for National Security to designate one federal prosecuting attorney who will not be considered a voting member.

(U) We reviewed HSRC minutes from 16 meetings conducted between February 2016 and November 2018 and found that for each HSRC meeting: (1) the FBI had only one of the two required FBI OGC attorneys; (2) the Department did not have a DAAG present from the Criminal Division for any of the meetings; (3) the number of additional federal prosecuting office attorneys participating in the meetings varied between one and three; and (4) there was no attorney designated by the AAG for National Security.

(U) We interviewed FBI and Department officials who participated in the HSRC process to gain an understanding of how the meetings functioned without a fullcompositionaccordingtoAG-Guidelines. Welearnedthroughtheseinterviews that two HSRC members-one Department official and one FBI official-generally decidedallHSRClong-termCHScontinueduserequests. BothFBI-andDepartment officials told us that that HSRC composition for the period we reviewed has left a few individuals assuming a large burden of risk and that, with the exception of the one Department official who shared in the decision-making burden, the other Department officials generally did not actively participate.

(U) The Criminal Division DMG to whom the Organized Crime and Gang Section reports told us that he was not aware of the AG Guidelines requirements for the composition of the HSRC, including the requirement for a DMG from the CriminalDivisiontoparticipate. We also interviewed the Chief of the Organized Crime and Gang Section who stated that having a Criminal Division DAAG participate in the HSRC was unnecessary. Headded that the DAAG would be more appropriate as an arbiter when consensus could not reached. Further, he believed that there should be more member participation but that the composition requirements should be reconsidered. Similarly, an FBI official who participates in the HSRC told us that the composition requirements should be revisited.

(U) We believe the Department and the FBI increased the risk of inadequate oversight of the FBI's long-term CHSs by placing an undue burden on a few HSRC membersratherthanthefullcomplementrequiredbytheAGGuidelines. We recommend that the Department and FBI coordinate to ensure the composition of the HSRC is sufficient and appropriate and includes the requisite skills and knowledge to approve the continued use of FBI's long-term CHSs and seek revisions to the AG Guidelines, as necessary, to memorialize any changes in the composition.

(U) HSRC Has a Backlog Which May Continue to Increase and Add to its Existing Burden

(U) As of September 2018, the FBI reported to us that there were 235 long termCHSsawaitingcontinueduseapprovalsfromtheHSRC. AccordingtotheFBI, the number had been reduced to 95 as of May 2019. However, as the FBI works to reduce the backlog of existing long-term CHS validations, this will inevitably increasetheburdenontheHSRCandpotentiallyaddtoitsbacklog. Inaddition,we tried to reconcile the decrease from 235 to 95 long-term CHSs awaiting review by theHSRCbasedonHSRCmeetingminutesandwefoundinconsistencies. Whenwe asked the FBI about these inconsistencies, we were informed that the numbers may not be exact due to Delta system errors or the fact that some CHSs did not meet the criteria for HSRC review.

(U) Nonetheless, we are concerned about the HSRC backlog for two primary reasons. First, as shown in Figure 1, we determined that between February 2016 and November 2018, the HSRC closed or added conditions-including caveats, questions, or recommendations-to 33 percent of the CHS files it reviewed.[61]

(U) Figure 1
(U) HSRC Meetings Results From February 2016 to November 2018

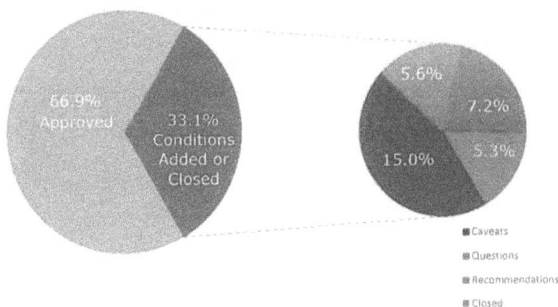

66.9%
Approved

33.1%
Conditions
Added or
Closed

5.6%

7.2%

15.0%

5.3%

■ Caveats
■ Questions
■ Recommendations
■ Closed

(U) Source: OIG based on FBI documentation.

(U) For example, we found in one review that the HSRC requested a CHS be closed because the CHS was a child sex offender, and the HSRC did not believe the benefitsofusingtheCHSoutweighedtheassociatedrisks. Inanotherinstance,the HSRC granted continued use approval but added a caveat that the CHS file be reviewedforunauthorizedillegalactivity. Further,inanotherinstancetheHSRC approved a CHS's continued use but added a recommendation to ensure SAC approval for continued use for five or more years is granted, an issue previously identified in this report. Because of the current backlogs of long-term CHSs awaiting both HSRC continued use determinations and FBI validations, these important con-

---

61 (U) According to HSRC minutes between February 2016 and November 2018, the HSRC applied the following conditions for CHSs continued use: (1) approving a CHS's continued use but adding a caveat which requires the handling agent to take a specific action; (2) approving a CHS's continued use based on a handling agent answering additional questions; and (3) approving a CHS's continued use while adding a recommendation for ongoing handling of the CHS. In addition, the HSRC also requested CHSs to be closed.

ditions or closures may not be added for significant periods of time.

(U) By not reviewing these long-term CHSs in a timely manner, we believe there is a risk that CHSs could remain active when they should have been closed or had additional conditions placed on their continued use.

(U) Our other concern regarding the HSRC backlog is, due to the frequency of the HSRC meetings and the number of long-term CHS files reviewed at each meeting, the HSRC will be unable to eliminate or even significantly reduce its long term CHS backlog. Between February 2016 and November 2018 (a period of 34 months), the HSRC met 16 times, as shown in Figure 2, making a total of 414 long term CHS continuing use decisions.

(U) Figure 2

(U) Long-Term CHSs Reviewed from February 2016 to November 2018

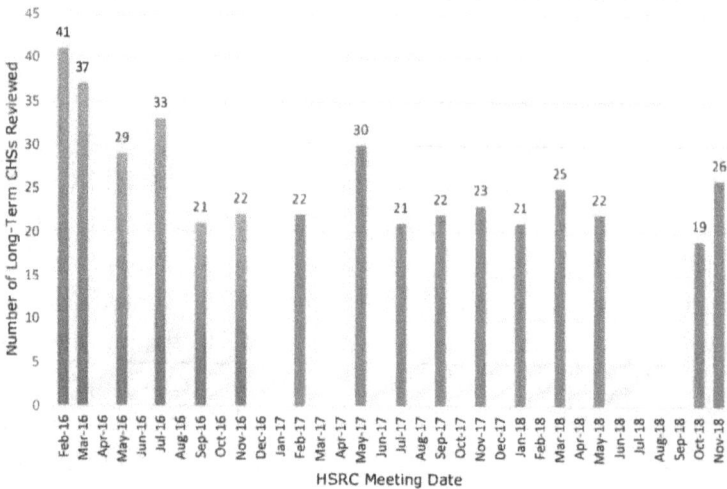

(U) The AG Guidelines do not specify the frequency that the HSRC should meet and we were told by HSRC members that more frequent meetings would be problematic given the preparation burden for each HSRC meeting. Although the HSRC met, on average, every other month between February 2016 and May 2018, we determined that the HSRC did not meet for a 4-month period between June 2018 and October 2018. We asked why no meetings were conducted during this time and were told that one of the two individuals who generally made continuing use decisions had been unable to attend the July 2018 meeting so it was cancelled. Subsequently, the September 2018 meeting was postponed due to a conflict with another event. We believe the cancellation of these meetings suggest that the HSRC has placed too much of the burden on a small number of individuals. These HSRC meetings are critical to the CHS program and every effort should be made to promptly reschedule them when they must be cancelled.

(U) According to Department and FBI officials, the HSRC can typically review no more than about 25 long-term CHS files at one meeting because of the burden involved in reviewing each file. A Department official told us that while the FBI was forwarding more than 25, it was too many for the HSRC to thoroughly review. The Department official stated that he informed the FBI that 25 long-term CHSs was the maximumnumbertheFBIshouldsendtotheHSRC. Whilelimitingthenumberof CHSs forwarded to the HSRC to 25 may be reasonable given the limited composition and burden involved in the preparation for each meeting, it suggests long-term CHS reviews are being delayed.

(U) Given that the HSRC added conditions to or closed about 33 percent of all long-term CHSs during continued use review, this oversight function appears to have merit and impact. Therefore, it is important that the HSRC operates consistently and without a backlog. And, although the HSRC has made some progress in reducing the backlog during this audit, we believe the Department and the FBI should consider convening additional HSRCs to mitigate the investigative and operational security risks associated with those long-term CHSs awaiting approvalforcontinueduse. AstheFBIworkstoreducethebacklogofexisting long-term CHS validations, this will inevitably increase the burden on the HSRC and potentially add to its backlog. As a result, the HSRC may continue to operate with an increasing backlog of continued use approvals if an alternative is not sought.

We recommend that the Department and FBI coordinate to consider establishing additional HSRCs or increasing the frequency of the HSRC meetings until the backlog of CHSs awaiting HSRC approval for continued use is eliminated.

(U) FBI Did Not Follow Its Policy Implementation Process When Revising Validation Practices

(U) The FBI's Internal Policy Office's (IPO) Policy Process Directive (IPO Directive) standardized the FBI's policy-making process to effectively coordinate, align, and deconflict policy-making activities and ensure compliance with laws, regulations, and applicable Department guidance. The IPO Directive also eliminated electronic communications as channels to create policy. According to the FBI,the IPO review process begins after the "owning division" submits the initial draft policy to the IPO.[62] This process is shown below in Figure 3.

(U) Figure 3
(U) FBI Policy Update Process

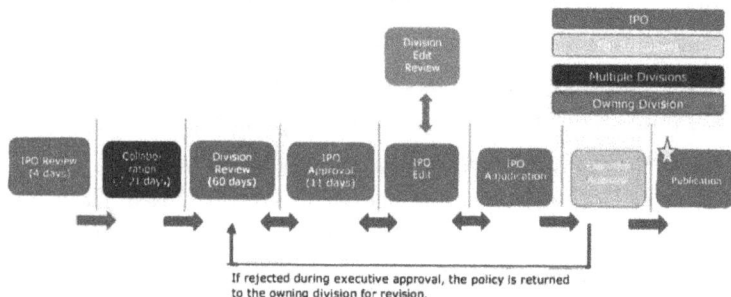

If rejected during executive approval, the policy is returned to the owning division for revision.

(U) We found that the DI changed its process for validating CHSs without following the process outlined above. Specifically, as described earlier, between 2011 and 2019, the DI implemented at least two different validation processes without incorporating them into policy. First, neither version of the CPS was incorporated into the Validation Manual. Instead, various electronic communications were issued to provide guidance on the process. In addition, in 2017, the DI developed a new validation process known as the Significant Source Review Panel process, which is discussed later in this report.

---

62 (U) An FBI "owning division" refers to the sponsoring entity submitting the policy. This can include both FBI headquarters divisions as well as field offices.

As with the CPS, the DI did not incorporate the Significant Source Review Panel process into policy and instead communicated it to FBI employees through the issuance of electronic communications. Because the DI did not incorporate these processes into policy, it missed the opportunity to go through the formal deconfliction process that should have identified its non-compliance with AG Guidelines requirements for long-term CHSs.

(U) As mentioned previously, the Inspection Division conducted a 2013 National Program Review. Although the 2013 National Program Review did not identify explicit non-compliance with the AG Guidelines, it observed that existing CHS policies were disjointed, inadequate, and out of date. Further, it highlighted that a draft Validation Manual was pending at the time of the 2013 National Program Review but had not been implemented. The 2013 National Program Review also reported that the Di's interactions with the IPO were not productive. IPO employees reported that a lack of engagement by the DI was a constant source of frustration and constituted "the single biggest policy risk to the FBI" at the time. As discussed previously, FBI officials told us that ongoing leadership turnover contributed to the Di's continuing challenges with formalizing policy.

(U) Over 2 months after our audit was initiated, DI leadership approved the issuance of an electronic communication that negated certain portions of the Validation Manual that had not been followed since at least 2015. For the reasons we note above, we do not believe this was an appropriate action to remedy the FBI's outdated validation policy because it circumvented the process for updating policy. In addition, by continuing to update processes through the issuance of electronic communications, the DI increases the risk of confusion and non compliance. WerecommendthattheDIupdateitsPolicyGuidetoformally incorporate its Validation Manual in accordance with the IPO Policy Directive to ensure current validation processes and procedures are in compliance with AG Guidelines requirements.

(U) FBI's Current Validation Process Lacks Adequate Independent Oversight and Should Be Reengineered

(U) We found that the FBI has not implemented adequate independent oversight in its current validation process, which creates a risk that CHSs are not adequately scrutinized or prioritized. As we discuss in the following paragraphs, the FBI's current validation process for significant CHSs did not provide sufficient independent FBI headquarters oversight and monitoring to ensure CHS risk is effectively mitigated.

(U) Implementation of the Significant Source Review Panel

(U) In February 2018, the FBI implemented a new validation process for its CHSs with characteristics the FBI believed were significant.[63] According to the FBI, the purpose of the new validation process was to: 1) improve the depth and relevancy of CHS validation, 2) offer FBI field offices the opportunity to understand and manage their own CHS risk, and 3) drive the validation process by field office proximity to significant cases rather than by CHS Prioritization System (CPS) score. The validation process, called the Significant Source Review Panel, is shown below in Figure 4.

(U) Figure 4
(U) Significant Source Review Panel

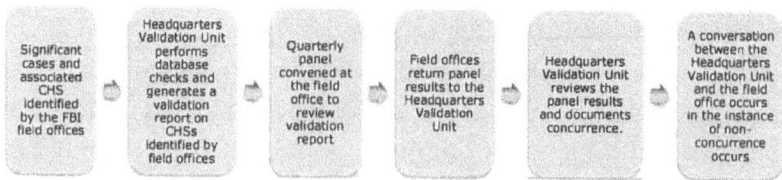

| Significant cases and associated CHS identified by the FBI field offices | Headquarters Validation Unit performs database checks and generates a validation report on CHSs identified by field offices | Quarterly panel convened at the field office to review validation report | Field offices return panel results to the Headquarters Validation Unit | Headquarters Validation Unit reviews the panel results and documents concurrence. | A conversation between the Headquarters Validation Unit and the field office occurs in the instance of non-concurrence occurs |

(U) According to the FBI, the process is initiated by field offices through the identification of significant cases and the CHSs associated with those cases.[64] The FBI provided a non-inclusive list of guidance to the field offic-

---

63 (U) The process was initiated as a pilot in five FBI field offices in March 2017 and implemented in all 56 field offices in February 2018.

64 (U) According to the FBI, a significant case may be one that: (1) is regularly briefed to FBI Executive Management or FBI headquarters; (2) involves sizable US government resources; or (3)

es to assist them in identifying significant CHSs for validation, including CHSs that may be:

- (U//FOUO) [REDACTED]
- (S//NF) [REDACTED]
- (U//FOUO) [REDACTED]
- (U//FOUO) [REDACTED]
- (S//NF) [REDACTED]
- (U//FOUO) [REDACTED]
- (S//NF) [REDACTED][65]

(U) As noted in Figure 4 above, significant CHSs are identified by and forwarded from the field office to the Validation Unit to conduct a CHS validation and issue a validation report.[66] The validation report is then provided to the field office where a panel is convened to review the report. After the panel concludes, it communicates its results to the Validation Unit for concurrence or non-concurrence. In the instance of non-concurrence, a discussion between the field office and the Validation Unit occurs.

(U) The OIG identified several deficiencies with the Significant Source Review Panel process. First, we determined that the guidance and messaging on the process was inadequate. Second, we found that the Validation Unit did not have a process in place to independently monitor and assess field office CHS selections for submission to the process and deferred to field offices concerning the continued CHS use. Lastly, we determined that Validation Unit Intelligence Analysts conducting validation reports were not authorized to 1) conduct analysis; 2) add caveats; or 3) draw conclusions or make recommendations, an issue previously described in this report with respect to long-term validation reports.

---

includes high level of violence.

65 (U) As noted earlier in this report, the FBI does not currently consider the length of use of a CHS as a significant risk factor.

66 (U) As part of the new validation process, the FBI developed a validation report called the Significant Source Validation Report.

(U) Significant Source Review Panel Guidance and Messaging Was Inadequate and Could Be Improved

(U) We determined that the Significant Source Review Panel process guidance and messaging was inadequate and, as a result, created confusion in the field offices. In addition, the guidance included subjective criteria for which CHSs should be forwarded to headquarters, leaving field offices with differing standards for CHS selection. Further, the FBI provided no evidence that certain field office personnelreceivedguidanceontheirrolesandresponsibilitiesintheprocess. At the time of this audit, CHS Coordinators, ASACs, and SSAs had received training on the process; however, we were not provided any documentation that handling agents and field office Division Counsels, among others, had received guidance and training.

(U) We were advised by an Assistant Division Counsel that those in her position had received no guidance about their role in the panel discussions, despite being asked to document their review. The same official told us that, due to the lack of guidance, the field office Chief Division Counsel told her not to sign off on the panel results. Further, despite being trained, a CHS Coordinator told us that the guidance was not clear about what CHS Coordinators were responsible for communicating to handling agents about the process. In addition, an SSA told us that FBI headquarters was not effective at explaining the process to the field offices. These statements were consistent with a December 2018 CHS validation process review conducted by the FBI's Resource Planning Office Internal Advisory Group that found, historically, changes to validation processes have not been effectively communicated to field offices.[67]

(U) Because the DI failed to provide adequate guidance and training to field office personnel participating in the process, we recommend that the FBI ensure all validation process roles and re-

---

67 (U) The FBI's Resource Planning Office Internal Advisory Group conducted a review of the FBI's CHS validation process. This review began in July 2018, 4 months after the initiation of the OIG's audit, to identify duplicative efforts in the CHS validation process and find efficiencies. The Internal Advisory Group presented its findings and recommendations to the DI in December 2018.

sponsibilities are defined and field office personnel receive adequate training on the validation processes.

(U) Significant Source Review Panel Process Should be Improved to Ensure Effective Independent Headquarters Oversight

(U) With the FBI's Significant Source Review Panel process, there is a risk that field offices may not identify their most significant CHSs for review. We asked FBI officials how they monitor field office selection and were told the DI did not have a process to assess field office CHS selection to ensure it met the guidance providedinvariouselectroniccommunications. Further,theValidationUnithadnot assessed the risks associated with allowing field offices to select CHSs for validation.

(U) Several FBI officials suggested to us that there is a risk that field offices may avoid the selection of certain CHSs for validation review because the field offices may wish to continue using those CHSs despite the presence of particular riskfactors. Infact,oneoftheseofficialstoldusthatthefieldofficesmaybe sending "softballs," meaning field offices may be sending CHSs lacking any significant risk factors. Another FBI official told us that given the field office's autonomy over the Significant Source Review Panel process, "there is no doubt that the field is picking their CHSs to avoid troublesome CHSs." If true, this could mean that the field offices may avoid validation review of the most risky CHSs, to ensure that they can continue using them. Although we did not conduct an assessment to determine whether field offices were intentionally withholding potentially concerning CHSs from validation review, we recognize the risk identified by the Intelligence Analysts and the FBI official and believe stronger internal controls should be considered.

(U) At the conclusion of the Significant Source Review Panel process, continued use determinations are made by the field office, and the results are forwardedtotheValidationUnitforconcurrenceornon-concurrence. Wereviewed the results from panels held from March 2017 through September 2018 and found that the

FBI conducted 718 panels across its 56 field offices.[68] Of these, 39 panels (or 5 percent) resulted in field offices closing the CHS. For the remaining 679 CHSs that the field office did not close, the Validation Unit granted concurrence in 100 percent of the panels. We believe that field office continuing use decisions, as with field office CHS selections, require closer scrutiny and oversight by the DI's Validation Unit.

(U) However, during our audit, the former Chief of the Validation Unit told us that he views the unit's role as supporting the field offices rather than providing oversight. This description of the Validation Unit's role mirrored the FBI's perspective discussed in a prior OIG review, which found that, within the FBI, there was belief that "the field was supreme and that FBI headquarters played a supporting role, having delegated virtually all authority to the field."[69] In response to that review, the FBI created validation entities "to implement a program with independent review capabilities." It now appears that the Validation Unit is deferring a significant amount of autonomy back to the field offices, thereby reducing its "independent review capabilities" and we believe this is further evidence of the Validation Unit moving back towards a supporting role. We discussed these concerns with the DI's Assistant Director who recognized that headquarters validation directives to the field have been an ongoing challenge for the FBI. We believe that the field office's autonomy in the Significant Source Review Panel process, from CHS selection to continued CHS use decisions, increases the likelihood that risks associated with CHSs will not be independently and objectively addressed and mitigated. We recommend the FBI reengineer its process for CHS validation to ensure that the CHSs with the greatest risk factors are selected, that those selections are independently assessed by headquarters, and that continued CHS use determinations receive appropriate headquarters scrutiny.

---

68 (U) These results include data from the period the process was initially piloted in five field offices.
69 (U) DOJ OIG, *A Review of the FBI's Handling and Oversight of FBI Asset Katrina Leung*, Oversight and Review Division Report (May 2006).

(U) Significant Source Validation Report Process Needs Improvement to Ensure Analysis, Conclusions, and Recommendations are Documented

(U) The Validation Manual states that the FBI has an abiding interest in establishing the validity of each CHS. Accordingly, the FBI has a duty to ensure that each CHS is reporting truthfully and to document those instances of red flags, derogatory reporting, and anomalies.

(U) However, we were told by multiple Intelligence Analysts that they received guidance to only state the facts and not to conduct analysis, report conclusions, and make recommendations in the Significant Source Review Panel validation reports. For example, one Intelligence Analyst told us that he was permitted to recommend a CHS receive a polygraph or operational test to the handling agent by phone but not permitted to document the recommendation in the CHS's validation report. Additionally, multiple FBI officials told us that they believe that field offices do not want negative information documented in a CHS file due to criminal discovery concerns and concerns about the CHS's ability to testify.[70] For example, one FBI official told us that some U.S. Attorney's offices will not use a CHS at trial if there is negative documentation in the CHS's file. However, a CHS Coordinator emphasized the historical value of documenting issues with the CHS because handling agents change and new handling agents can only know the risks if they are documented.

(U) A prior 2013 OIG review found that FBI headquarters validation personnel could make one of three recommendations with respect to a CHS: continue to operate, continue to operate with caveats, or close.[71] We believe that these important recommendations

---

70 (U) Validation documents relevant to the credibility of a CHS may be discoverable in judicial proceedings. Discovery in criminal cases is controlled by case law and the Federal Rules of Criminal Procedure. For example, information in the validation report which refers to the CHS's motivation or vulnerabilities may be discoverable pursuant to *Brady v. Maryland*, 373 U.S. 83 {1963} or *Giglio v. United States*, 405 U.S. 150 {1972}. "Brady" refers to information known to the government that is material to a criminal case and could tend to exculpate the defendant. "Giglio" refers to information that could be used to impeach a witness for the prosecution.

71 (U) DOJ OIG, *A Review of the FBI's Progress in Responding to the Recommendations in the DIG Report on the FBI's Handling and Oversight of Katrina Leung* (October 2013).

should continue as they serve an important independentoversight-function. Inaddition,bywithholdingpotentiallycritical information from validation reports, the FBI runs the risks that (1) prosecutors may not have complete and reliable information when a CHS serves as a witness and, thus, may have difficulties complying with their discovery obligations; and (2) future handling agents may be deprived of relevant information about the CHS that could not only jeopardize an investigation but also put the agent's safety and potentiallysensitiveinformationatrisk. WerecommendtheFBIensuresthat headquarters validation personnel document their analyses, conclusions, and recommendations in validation reports.

(U) FBI's Annual CHS Validation Report and the Communication of its Importance Should be Improved

(U) The AG Guidelines require that each CHS file receive a validation at least annually by the FBI. To address this requirement, the FBI's Validation Manual states that ASACs are responsible for reviewing annual CHS reports, which are then forwarded to headquarters for an independent review to ensure completeness and to determine the level of validation a CHS receives.

(U//FOUO) However, we found that the FBI was not following its own guidance for annual CHS validations in that annual reports are no longer reviewed byheadquartersvalidationpersonnel. As noted previously, in April 2018, over 2 months after the OIG initiated this audit, the Di's Assistant Director approved a departure from certain requirements of the Validation Manual, including the independent headquarters validation unit reviews of annual CHS reports. Although the Assistant Director granted approval, the departure was never formalized as policy. An FBI official told us that it was not feasible to conduct reviews of all annual CHS reports because of the limited number of validation personnel. Given the FBI's current validation resources and an active CHS base of over [REDACTED], we agree with this assessment. In our view, with appropriate guidance to handling agents on preparing a well-designed annual CHS report and to ASACs on how to review them, we believe the ASAC review of the annual CHS reports can be sufficient to satisfy the AG Guidelines requirements.

(U) Although we believe reviews by ASACs could satisfy minimum AG Guidelines requirements, we identified areas of the reporting process that should be strengthened. For example, we were told that FBI handling agents often cut and paste information from prior annual reports into the revised reports. This can inadvertently lead to the carrying forward of duplicative and outdated information. Some FBI officials attributed this to the FBI not adequately communicating the importance of the annual report in the FBI's CHS validation process.

(U) The FBI Inspection Division's 2013 National Program Review also identified issues related to the annual CHS report. Specifically, the 2013 National Program Review found that field offices did not understand the annual CHS report's role or importance in the CHS validation process and reported that nearly 43 percent of the 2,101 agents who responded to the survey indicated the annual report was not effective in identifying CHS risks. To address this issue, the Inspection Division recommended that the DI disseminate guidance to the field offices highlighting the annual CHS report as a fundamental component of validation and develop a training module illustrating how it can mitigate risk. We asked the DI how it addressed this recommendation but it could not provide us with any evidence that this internal recommendation had been implemented. Furthermore, the FBI's December 2018 Resource Planning Office review of the FBI's validation process noted that some questions on the current annual CHS report are duplicative and may not sufficiently address the highest priority risks.

(U) We believe that a poorly designed annual CHS report may fail to sufficiently identify the CHS risks. In addition, given the important role the annual CHS report plays in the validation process, we believe it is critical that the importance of this report is adequately communicated to all FBI field offices. We recommend that the FBI

(1) update its Validation Manual to ensure that its annual CHS review process is accurately documented; and (2) review and update its annual CHS report to ensure that it sufficiently addresses CHS risks, provide field offices guidance on the updates, and stress to field offices the importance of the annual CHS report in the FBI's validation process.

(U) Challenges Exist in Securing and Safeguarding CHS Communications and Information

(U) Safely communicating and securely documenting contact with CHSs are critical aspects of the FBI's intelligence gathering process. We identified two areas where the FBI could improve its guidance and controls in this area.

(U) FBI Lacked Clear Policy for Communications with CHSs and Should Develop Policies for Acceptable Communication Platforms

(U) Secure communications are vital to the operational security of FBI investigationsacrossallFBIprograms. Failuretousesecurecommunicationscan allow for the interception and exploitation of highly sensitive information by adversaries and potentially compromise the safety of FBI personnel as well as CHSs. Although the FBI's Policy Guide discourages agents from using email, text message, facsimile, and other electronic communications when communicating with CHSs,itdoesnotprohibitthem. Further,thepolicydoesnotpositivelyidentifythe types of devices, applications, and methods that should be used when communicating with CHSs to mitigate operational and safety risks.

(U) Overall, we found varying uses of communication platforms among FBI handling agents. SomehandlingagentsusedtheirFBI issued devices, while others used non FBI-issued devices to communicate with their CHSs. The disparity in type of device used appeared to be based on a number of factors, including: (1) the handling agent's field office, (2) the handling agent's operational division, (3) the handling agent's supervisor, (4) the ease of obtaining non-FBI-issued devices within the field office, and (5) the experience of the handling agent.

(U//FOUO) [REDACTED]

(S//NF) During our audit we learned that the FBI has an ongoing initiative related to the FBI-wide use of technology when communicating with CHSs. The purpose of the initiative is to identify and assess the FBI's vulnerabilities and operational risks to better ensure secure communication methods and contacts with CHSs. This internal initiative included a surve which found [REDACTED].[72] Nearly [REDACTED] of the survey's respondents stated that they had never received formal training on communicating with CHSs or that the training they had received was inadequate. The team leading this FBI initiative also determined that the FBI lacks clear and concise guidance on communicating with CHSs.

> (U) FIELD OFFICE QUOTES
>
> (U) "The FBI has no policy guidance for non attributable device use for when communicating with CHSs, which increases the operational security risks."
>
> (U) "No FBI policy prohibits the use of government phones to communicate with CHSs, so many agents use their bureau phones."
>
> (U) "It is critical to make the first contact [with a CHS] with a non attributable device...[although] no policy requires non attributable devices."

(U) Despite the lack of clear guidance for CHS communications, we did identify some field offices where a supervisor or specific unit encouraged techniques that may have reduced the operational risks associated with CHSs communications. For example, one SSA told us that he does not allow any of his agents to use FBI issueddevice-stocommunicatewithCHSsbecauseofthesecurityrisks. Another FBI official who is responsible for HUMINT training told us that despite the absence of official policy, the FBI's HUMINT Operations Training Unit trains handling agents not to use FBI-issued devices when communicating with CHSs.

(U) Because of the importance and sensitivity of many of the FBI's law enforcement, national security, and intelligence operations, as

---

72 (U) According to FBI documentation, the initiative team surveyed 49 field offices and 14 Legal Attaché offices and received a total of 508 responses.

well as the risks to both FBI personnel and CHSs, we recommend that the FBI develop and implement a policy that clearly informs FBI personnel of the acceptable platforms for communicating with CHSs and provides training to its workforce on the policy.

(U) Ensuring Highly Classified CHS Reporting is Properly Safeguarded

(SI/NF) We found the FBI was not ensuring its highly classified CHS documentationwassafeguardedfrompotentialunauthorized-access. Durin audit the FBI used a shared site called [REDACTED]

(U//FOUO) According to the policy guide, [REDACTED].[73] [REDACTED] did not possess the requisite "need to know." As of September 2018, the FBI [REDACTED]. When we discussed this concern with FBI officials, they told us that DI leadership was considering alternatives to [REDACTED]. In addition, we were told that the DI is no longer promoting the use of [REDACTED] to the field offices and it will be phased out once the new system is operational.

(U//FOUO) [REDACTED] system can be potentially accessed by those without a specific "need to know," [REDACTED], the FBI should ensure unathorized access [REDACTED]. We recommend that the DI restrict access to its highly classified CHS shared system to only those with a need to know until the system is replaced.

(U) FBI Should Prioritize Automation of its Processes to Identify and Fill Gaps in CHS Coverage

(U) In addition to ensuring an adequate CHS base, the FBI must align its CHSs with its highest threat priorities to better ensure the security and safety of the American public. In order to succeed in that effort, the FBI must continually assess its CHS placement and access to detect any gaps in its CHS coverage.

(U) Inefficient Process for Assessing CHS Coverage and Identifying Potential Gaps

---

73 (U) As noted earlier, Delta is the FBI's primary CHS management system. However, it is not approved for all classification levels.

(S//NF) As of April 2018, the FBI had [REDACTED] intelligence gaps ranging from groups [REDACTED]. However, we found that the FBI lacked an automated process to analyze its CHS coverage to address these gaps and relied on an ineffective process that was time consuming andresultedinpotentiallyobsoleteinformation. Specifically,welearnedthatFBI Collection Managers must manually combine data from separate FBI systems into spreadsheets to identify its most up-to-date CHS coverage. According to one FBI official, this inefficient process can produce information that is immediately outdated. We agree that this process is inefficient and can yield stale information and, further, we believe the process is prone to human error because of the manual entry required. FBI officials told us that they are aware of these deficiencies and described a new threat intelligence and CHS coverage system being developed to automatethisprocess. At the time of our audit, the FBI forecasted that the new system would be deployed in the summer of 2019. We recommend that the FBI take actions to mitigate its gaps in CHS coverage by prioritizing the development of its new threat intelligence and CHS coverage system and ensure that the policies and procedures for its use are documented and accompanied by detailed training on the new system.

(U) FBI Should Ensure Data Integrity of Underlying Systems for its Proposed Threat Intelligence and CHS Coverage System

(U) While we believe an automated threat intelligence and CHS coverage system is a step in the right direction for the FBI to more efficiently and effectively understand its CHS coverage, we found that the proposed system relies on ingesting data from several other FBI systems, including Delta. As we have already noted, we have significant concerns with the quality of the information in Delta.

(U) We discussed our concerns with the FBI officials responsible for developing the new automated system and provided them with examples of data issuesidentifiedduringouraudit. Inoneinstance-aSSAtoldusthattaggingCHS threatsinDeltaisconfusingandshould-besimplified. Thissupervisorbelievedthat many agents "just hit the buttons to get the form to move onto the next screen" withoutregardtotheaccuracyoftheinformationtheyinput. Inaddition,wewere told that some data fields in Delta are not mandatory and that many agents will skipadatafieldifitisnotmandatory. Whenweaskedwhycertainfieldswerenot mandatory in Delta, an FBI official told us that the DI does not want to overburden agentswithpolicyrequirements. WealsofoundthatbecauseDeltadoesnot identify and track extraterritorial sub-sources, the proposed CHS coverage system will lack complete and accurate information on its CHS coverage stemming from extraterritorial sub-sources.[74]

(U) We learned that in September 2018, the FBI initiated a Delta data assessment conducted by a FBI contractor to identify Delta's areas of incomplete, incorrect, or missing data. The assessment concluded in January 2019 and results of the assessment included a recommendation to the FBI to improve Delta's data quality as well as findings such as:

- Certain fields were not enforced, which may lead to unpreditable results;
- Reduntant data existed in multiple locations within Delta; and
- Incorrect data.

(U) Without complete and reliable information in its underlying systems, the FBI's proposed system cannot accurately identify intelligence gaps and CHS coverage. We believe that remedying Delta's data quality issues will assist the FBI indevelopingamorereliablethreatintelligenceandCHScoverageplatform. We recommend that the FBI consult with all proposed stakeholders that will be responsible for providing data to the new system, identify any other data integrity issues, and document the policies and procedures for ongoing data quality monitoring of its new threat intelligence and CHS coverage system.

---

74 (U) A sub-source is any individual who directly acquires information that is then provided to the FBI by an FBI CHS.

(U) CONCLUSION AND RECOMMENDATIONS

(U) We identified issues related to aspects of the FBI's oversight and management of its FBI's CHS program. First, regarding long-term CHSs, we found that the FBI failed to comply with AG Guidelines' validation requirements and its own validation policies and procedures, and maintained a significant backlog of long-termCHSsawaitingvalidation. Relatedtothisfinding,wealsoidentified issues with the FBI's long-term CHS validation reports, insufficient validation resources, and inadequately trained personnel who conduct these reviews. In addition, we found that the FBI lacked an automated process to identify, track, and monitor its long-term CHSs or to document continued agent handling approvals in FBI field offices. We believe these issues increased the likelihood that some of the risksassociatedwithlong-termCHSswerelikelynotmitigated. Secondandalso concerning long-term CHSs, we found that the joint DOJ and FBI HSRC consistently fell short of the composition requirements of the AG Guidelines, placing continued use approval decisions on a few rather than the full complement of personnel contemplated by the AG Guidelines. This contributed to an additional backlog of long-term CHSs awaiting continuing use determinations and increased the risk that long-term CHSs continued to operate when they should have been closed or had important conditions added to their continued use. Third, because the FBI changed its process for validating CHSs without following its own directives for incorporating new processes and procedures into policy, it missed an opportunity to go through the formal deconfliction process that should have identified its non-compliance with AG Guidelines requirements for long-term CHSs. Fourth, we determined that the FBI's current validation process lack sufficient independent headquarters oversight and monitoring. Fifth, FBI's annual CHS report may not be sufficiently addressing CHS risk. Sixth, we identified areas that could be improved related to CHS communications. Finally,we found that the FBI was in the process of developing a system to align its CHSs with its highest threat priorities. However, we determined that the proposed system relies on utilizing data from several other FBI systems, including its Delta system, which has known data quality issues. ongoing data quality monitoring of its new threat intelligence and CHS coverage system.

(U) We recommend the FBI:

1. (U) Ensure that the DI designs, implements, and adheres to validation policies and procedures for its long-term CHSs that comply with the AG Guidelines, or coordinate with the Department to seek revisions to the AG Guidelines, as necessary.
2. (U) Dedicate sufficient and appropriately trained personnel to ensure that long-term CHS validations, including backlogged long-term CHS validations, are conducted in accordance with the requirements of the AG Guidelines.
3. (U) Coordinate with the Department and update, as necessary, its long term CHS validation report to ensure that it addresses the appropriate scope of review and memorializes any validation personnel's conclusions or recommendations.
4. (U) Develop and implement an automated mechanism in its Delta system to ensure that long-term CHSs are accurately identified and monitored, including an automated notification to the headquarters unit responsible for conducting long-term CHS validations.
5. (U) Develop and implement an automated workflow in Delta to ensure that all handling agents request and document SAC approval or disapproval for the continued handling of CHSs in excess of 5 years.
6. (U) Update its Policy Guide to formally incorporate its Validation Manual in accordance with the IPO Policy Directive to ensure current validation processes and procedures are in compliance with AG Guidelines requirements.
7. (U) Ensure all validation process roles and responsibilities are defined and field office personnel receive adequate training on the validation processes.

8. (U) Reengineer its process for CHS validation to ensure that the CHSs with the greatest risk factors are selected, that those selections are independently assessed by headquarters, and that continued CHS use determinations receive appropriate headquarters scrutiny.

9. (U) Ensure that headquarters validation personnel document their analyses, conclusions, and recommendations in validation reports.

10. (U) Update its Validation Manual to ensure that its annual CHS review process is accurately documented and review and update its annual CHS report to ensure that it sufficiently addresses CHS risks, provide field offices guidance on the updates, and stress to field offices the importance of the annual CHS report in the FBI's validation process.

11. (U) Develop and implement a policy that clearly informs FBI personnel of the acceptable platforms for communicating with CHSs and provide training to its workforce on the policy.

12. (U) Restrict access to its highly classified CHS shared system to only those with a need to know until the system is replaced.

13. (U) Take actions to mitigate its gaps in CHS coverage by prioritizing the development of its new threat intelligence and CHS coverage system and ensure that the policies and procedures for its use are documented and accompanied by detailed training on the new system.

14. (U) Consult with all proposed stakeholders that will be responsible for providing data to the new system, identify any other data integrity issues, and document the policies and procedures for ongoing data quality monitoring of its new threat intelligence and CHS coverage system.

(U) We recommend the Department and FBI:

15. (U) Coordinate to ensure the composition of the HSRC is sufficient and appropriate and includes the requisite skills and knowledge to approve the continued use of FBI's long-term CHSs and seek revisions to the AG Guidelines, as necessary,

to memorialize any changes in the composition.

16. (U) Coordinate to consider establishing additional HSRCs or increasing the frequency of the HSRC meetings until the backlog of CHSs awaiting HSRC approval for continued use is eliminated.

(U) STATEMENT ON INTERNAL CONTROLS

(U) As required by the Government Auditing Standards, we tested, as appropriate, internal controls significant within the context of our audit objectives. A deficiency in an internal control exists when the design or operation of a control does not allow management or employees, in the normal course of performing their assigned functions, to timely prevent or detect: (1) impairments to the effectiveness and efficiency of operations, (2) misstatements in financial or performance information, or (3) violations of laws and regulations. Our evaluation of the FBI's internal controls was not made for the purpose of providing assurance on its internal control structure as a whole. FBI management is responsible for the establishment and maintenance of internal controls.

(U) As noted in the Audit Results section of this report, we identified deficiencies in the FBI's internal controls that are significant within the context of the audit objectives and based upon the audit work performed that we believe may adversely affect the FBI's ability to adequately manage the risks associated with operating CHSs.

(U) Because we are not expressing an opinion on the FBI's internal control structure as a whole, this statement is intended solely for the information and use of the FBI. This restriction is not intended to limit the distribution of this report, which is a matter of public record. However, we are limiting the distribution of this report because it contains sensitive information that must be appropriately controlled.[41]

---

41 (U) A redacted copy of this report with sensitive information removed will be made available publicly.

(U) STATEMENT ON COMPLIANCE WITH LAWS AND REGULATIONS

(U) As required by the Government Auditing Standards, we tested, as appropriate given our audit scope and objectives, selected records, procedures, and practices to obtain reasonable assurance that the FBI's management complied with federal laws and regulations for which noncompliance, in our judgment, could have a material effect on the results of our audit. FBI's management is responsible for ensuring compliance with applicable federal laws and regulations. In planning our audit, we identified the following regulation that concerned the operations of the auditee and that were significant within the context of the audit objectives:

- Attorney General Guidelines Regarding the Use of FBI Confidential Human Sources

(U) Our audit included examining, on a test basis, the FBI's compliance with the aforementioned laws and regulations that could have a material effect on the FBI's operations, through interviewing FBI personnel, analyzing data, examining practices, and assessing internal control procedures. As noted in the Audit Results section of this report, we found that the FBI did not comply with aspects of the Attorney General Guidelines Regarding the Use of FBI Confidential Human Sources.

(U) APPENDIX 1
(U) OBJECTIVES, SCOPE, AND METHODOLOGY

(U) Objectives

(U) The objectives of the audit were to (1) evaluate the FBI's CHS program policies and procedures, including its validation procedures; (2) assess the FBI's policies and practices for the use of non-attributable communications between agents and CHSs; and (3) examine the FBI's ability to identify and fill gaps in the alignment of its CHSs with the nation's highest priority threats and intelligence needs.

(U) Scope and Methodology

(U) We conducted this performance audit in accordance with generally accepted government auditing standards. Those standards require that we plan and perform the audit to obtain sufficient, appropriate evidence to provide a reasonable basis for our findings and conclusions based on our audit objectives.

We believe that the evidence obtained provides a reasonable basis for our finding and conclusions based on our audit objectives. Our audit of FBI's CHS program generally covered, but was not limited to, FY 2012 through activities that took place through May 2019.

(U) To evaluate the FBI's CHS program policies and procedures, including validation practices, we interviewed over 100 FBI officials, including individuals from the FBI's Criminal Investigative Division, Counterintelligence Division, Counterterrorism Division, Directorate of Intelligence, Information Technology Applications and Data Division, Insider Threat Office, Inspection Division, Office of Professional Responsibility, Resource Planning Office, and Weapons of Mass Destruction Directorate. In addition, we conducted site visits and interviewed responsible officials at FBI field offices in Philadelphia, Pennsylvania and Washington, D.C. We also interviewed officials from the U.S. Department of Justice Criminal and National Security Divisions and officials from another US Intelligence Community agency.

(U) We reviewed guidelines and policy documents, including the December 2006 Attorney Guidelines Regarding the Use of FBI Confidential Human Sources, the FBI's September 2015 CHS Policy Guide, and the March 2010 CHS Validation Standards Manual to gain an understanding of the policies and procedures in place during' the scope of this audit.

(U) During our review, we obtained information from the FBI's Delta system. We did not test the reliability of the Delta system as a whole, therefore any findings identified involving information from those systems were verified with documentation from other sources. As noted in our report, FBI officials expressed concerns about the data quality of Delta and a Delta Data Assessment study was conducted during our audit to identify Delta's areas of incomplete, incorrect, or missing data. This assessment identified issues in the Delta's data and structure which created challenges for accessing and using the data and found that duplicative, incomplete, and malformed data exists. We noted exceptions related tothereliability-oftheDeltadatathroughoutthereport. Inaddition,whilewe attempted to obtain data from Delta to quantify the FBI's long-term CHS backlog issue from FY2011 through FY 2018, we were told that the numbers we received could not be relied upon. Therefore, we did not use the data we received for that time period and did not rely on Delta's data for the basis for our findings.

(U) CHS Communication

(U) To assess the FBI's CHS communication practices, we reviewed FBI policy guidanceonCHScommunications. Inaddition,wemetwithFBIofficialstasked with reviewing policies the FBI has in place governing the communications with CHSsaspartofanongoingdigitaloperationssecurityinitiative. Further,wemet with FBI officials related to the storage and safeguarding of highly classified CHS communications and reviewed documents related to the system.

(U) CHS Coverage

(U) To examine the FBI's ability to identify and fill gaps, we interviewed FBI officials tasked with the development of the FBI's automated CHS coverage platform as well as received a demonstration and reviewed documentation on the proposed system. In addition, we reviewed policy directives and guidance related to collection management, including the FBI's Intelligence Program Policy Directive and Policy Guide.

(U) We also reviewed the FBI's January 2019 Delta Data Assessment to gain an understanding of the effect of the quality of Delta's data on its proposed CHS coverage platform. As noted in the Audit Results, the Delta Data Assessment found issues in the data and structure that created challenges for accessing and using the data of Delta.

(U) APPENDIX 2
(U) Prior Reports

(U)The OIG identified several prior reviews. Below we discuss these reviews and the status of corrective actions taken by the FBI to address recommendations in these reviews.

(U) Office of the Inspector General Reviews

(U) The FBI's Compliance with the Attorney General's Investigative Guidelines

(U) In September 2005, the OIG completed a review of The FBI's Compliance with the Attorney General's Investigative Guidelines.[42] Among the most significant issues identified during the review included failures by the FBI to comply with the 2002 Attorney General's Guidelines Regarding the Use of Confidential Informants.[43] As a result of the this review, the FBI began developing its Delta system, an automated CHS database intended to (1) facilitate the CHS management by automating manual workflows; (2) expand the ability to search intelligence obtainedfromCHSs;and(3)reduce-paperworkandhumanerror. Delta was officially launched in 2008 and all recommendations from the review have been implemented.

(U) A Review of the FBI's Handling and Oversight of FBI Asset Katrina Leung

(U) In May 2006, the OIG completed A Review of the FBI's Handling and Oversight of FBI Asset Katrina Leung.[44] The review included the FBI's handling of Katrina Leung, one of the FBI's highest paid, long-term counterintelligence CHSs who allegedly also worked for the People's Republic of China, and the performance and management issues relating to her case. The OIG concluded

---

42 (U) U.S. Department of Justice, Office of the Inspector General, *The FBI's Compliance with the Attorney General's Investigative Guidelines* (September 2005).

43 (U) The May 2002 AG Guidelines Regarding the Use of Confidential Informants were superseded by the current 2006 AG Guidelines Regarding the Use of FBI Confidential Human Sources.

44 (U) DOJ OIG, *A Review of the FBI's Progress in Responding to the Recommendations in the OIG Report on the FBI's Handling and Oversight of Katrina Leung* (October 2013).

that the FBI's inattention to oversight and supervisory mismanagement permitted the long-term CHS access to sensitive FBI information and to engage in an intimate relationship with her handling agent, both of which continued over an 18 year period. The review made 11 recommendations, including recommendations to improve FBI CHS validationproceduresandpractices. Asdiscussedbelow,afollow-upreviewwas conducted to evaluate the FBI's progress in responding to the OIG's 11 recommendations.

(U) A Review of the FBI's Progress in Responding to the Recommendations in the OIG Report on the FBI's Handling and Oversight of Katrina Leung

(U) In October 2013, the OIG completed A Review of the FBI's Progress in Responding to the Recommendations in the OIG Report on the FBI's Handling and Oversight of Katrina Leung, a follow-up review of the 2006 Katrina Leung Review.[45] The 2013 review found that the FBI had implemented 5 of the 11 recommendations from the 2006 Katrina Leung Review and, as shown in Table 1 below. In October 2015, the FBI provided the OIG responses to the 6 remaining recommendations and those recommendations remained on hold/pending with OIG as of August 2019.[46]

---

45 (U) DOJ OIG, *A Review of the FBI's Progress in Responding to the Recommendations in the OIG Report on the FBI's Handling and Oversight of Katrina Leung* (October 2013).
46 (U) The term "On Hold/Pending with OIG" means the completion of the OIG's assessment of the status of the recommendation is on hold or pending due to ongoing reviews or other factors.

2006 Katrina Leung Review Recommendation Number	Status	Recommendation
1	On Hold/Pending with OIG	The FBI should continue its FBI Headquarters managed asset validation review process and provide sufficient resources for the Analytical Unit to devote to these reviews.
2	On Hold/Pending with OIG	The FBI should require that any analytical products relating to the asset, together with red flags, derogatory reporting, anomalies, and other counterintelligence concerns be documented in a subsection of the asset's file.
3	On Hold/Pending with OIG	The FBI should require the field Supervisory Special Agent, the Assistant Special Agent in Charge, and the FBI Headquarters Supervisory Special Agent responsible for each asset to signify that they have reviewed the entries in this [Validation] subsection as part of the routine file review or of semi-annual or annual asset re-evaluations. If anomalies exist, the Supervisory Special Agent should note what action has been taken with respect to them, or explain why no action is necessary, and the Assistant Special Agent's in- Charge agreement should be noted.

2006 Katrina Leung Review Recommendation Number	Status	Recommendation
6	On Hold/Pending with OIG	The FBI should require agents to record in the asset I file any documents passed and all matters discussed with the asset, as well as each person who was present for the meeting.
7	On Hold/Pending with OIG	The FBI should require alternate case agents to meet with the source on a regular basis, together with the case agent.
8	On Hold/Pending with OIG	The FBI should limit the number of years any Special Agent can continue as an asset's handler. Exceptions should be allowed for good cause only.

(U) Source: OIG

(U) Federal Bureau of Investigation's Inspection Division Reviews

(U) In addition to OIG reviews, we identified FBI Inspection Division reviews and inspections related to the recruitment, handling, and use of CHSs. These reviews and inspections included observations of issues that were significant within the objectives of this audit and we discuss these reviews further in the following paragraphs.

<u>(U) Confidential Human Source National Program Review</u>

(U) In 2013, the FBI's Inspection Division conducted a CHS National Program Review. This review made 13 observations that resulted in 26 recommendations to the DI and other FBI branches and divisions.[41] According to the FBI's Inspection Division, all rec-

---

41 (U) The FBI Inspection Division used the term observation throughout its 2013 CHS National Program Review to describe an area of non-compliance within the FBI's CHS program.

---

ommendations from the review have been implemented. However, as noted throughout the Audit Results section of this report, we found instances where observations made by the Inspection Division persist or were not fully implemented.

(U) FBI Field Office Inspections

(U) The FBI's Inspection Division conducts periodic reviews of its field offices to assess their compliance with 14 different program areas, including CHS Performance. In FY2017, the Inspection Division reviewed 12 field office CHS programs (or 21 percent of the 56 field offices) and documented over 100 observations related to the CHS programs at those field offices. The most frequently observed area of non-compliance was inadequate quarterly and annual CHS reports.

(U) APPENDIX 3
(U) FEDERAL BUREAU OF INVESTIGATION'S RESPONSE TO THE DRAFT AUDIT REPORT

U.S. Department of Justice

Federal Bureau of Investigation

Washington, D. C. 20535-0001

September 24, 2019

The Honorable Michael E. Horowitz
Inspector General
Office of the Inspector General
U.S. Department of Justice
950 Pennsylvania Avenue, N.W.
Washington, DC 20530

Dear Mr. Horowitz:

The Federal Bureau of Investigation (FBI) appreciates the opportunity to review and respond to your office's report entitled, *Audit of the Federal Bureau of Investigation's Management of its Confidential Human Source Validation Processes.*

The Human Source Review Committee (HSRC) comprised of DOJ and FBI has had a positive impact as 33% of the CHS files reviewed between February 2016 and November 2018 were closed, or continued operation with conditions added including caveats or recommendations. The FBI looks forward to improving the HSRC in order to address the highest risk CHSs in a timely manner.

We agree it is important to continue to improve the validation process to ensure compliance with the AG Guidelines. The FBI has already initiated meetings with DOJ to address possible revisions to the AG Guidelines to establish a better validation policy with a cohesive CHS validation strategy. In that regard, we concur with your fourteen recommendations for the FBI and the two recommendations for the Department and FBI.

Should you have any questions, feel free to contact me. We greatly appreciate the professionalism of your audit staff throughout this matter.

Sincerely,

Suzanne Turner
Section Chief
External Audit and Compliance Section
Inspection Division

Enclosure

(U) The FBI's Response to the Office ofthe Inspector General's Audit ofthe Federal Bureau ofInvestigation's Management ofits Confidential Human Source Validation Processes

(U)Recommendation 1: OIG recommends FBI ensure that the DI designs, implements, and adheres to validation policies and procedures for its long-term CHSs that comply with the AG Guidelines, or coordinate with the Department to seek revisions to the AG Guidelines, as necessary.

(U) FBI Response to Recommendation 1: Concur. The FBI has already initiated meetings with DOJ to address possible revisions to the AG Guidelines that would better align current FBI resources, personnel, and policies with a cohesive long-term CHS validation strategy. The FBI is assessing other characteristics that might indicate higher risk levels and a need for enhanced scrutiny, as opposed to utilizing long-term continuous handling as the sole criteria for enhanced review. The CHS Policy Guide is in the process of being updated to reflect the most recent changes to the FBI's current validation process, to include the results of the above-mentioned assessment and any resulting changes to the AG Guidelines.

(U)Recommendation 2: OIG recommends FBI dedicate sufficient resources to ensure that long-term CHS validations, including backlogged long-term CHS validations, are conducted in accordance with the requirements ofthe AG Guidelines.

(U) FBI Response to Recommendation 2: Concur. The FBI has already initiated meetings with DOJ to address possible revisions to the AG Guidelines that would better align current FBI resources, personnel, and policies with a cohesive long-term CHS validation strategy. The FBI will evaluate resources and the process to ensure long-term validations to include the back log are conducted in accordance with the requirements of the AG Guidelines.

(U)Recommendation 3: OIG recommends FBI coordinate with the Department and update, as necessary, its long-term CHS validation report to ensure that it addresses the appropriate scope of review and memorializes any validation personnel's conclusions or recommendations.

(U) FBI Response to Recommendation 3: Concur. The FBI has already initiated meetings with DOJ to address possible revisions to the AG Guidelines that would better align current FBI resources, personnel, and policies with a cohesive long-term CHS validation strategy. This would potentially result in a new validation product with a new set ofparameters for period of review, depth of analysis, and responsible personnel. Furthermore, the inclusion of recommendations and conclusions in the validation report will be discussed with DOJ and internally with OGC.

(U)Recommendation 4: OIG recommends FBI develop and implement anautomated mechanism in its Delta system to ensure that long-term CBSs are accurately identified and monitored, including an automated notification to the headquarters unit responsible for conducting long-term CHS validations.

(U) FBI Response to Recommendation 4: Concur. The automated mechanism in the Delta system to ensure long-term CHSs are accurately identified and monitored to include a notification to headquarters was deployed in 08/2019 and is currently being tested to ensure accuracy.

(U)Recommendation5: OIGrecommendsFBIdevelopandimplementanautomated workflow in Delta to ensure that all handling agents request and document SAC approval or disapproval for the continued handling of CHSs in excess of 5 years.

(U) FBI Response to Recommendation 5: Concur. The FBI is currently working on automating the SAC approval or disapproval for continued handling of a CHS in excess of 5 years and is tentatively scheduled for deployment in Quarter 2 of FY 2020.

(U)Recommendation 6: OIG recommends FBI update its Policy Guide to formally incorporate its Validation Manual in accordance with the IPO Policy Directive to ensure current validation processes and procedures are in compliance with AG Guidelines requirements.

(U) FBI Response to Recommendation 6: Concur. The FBI is currently working to update the CHS Validation Manual (CHSVM) and to fully incorporate it into the CHS Policy Guide (CHSPG). The policy guide will ensure compliance with the AG Guidelines.

(U)Recommendation 7: OIGrecommendsFBIensureallvalidationprocessrolesand responsibilities are defined and field office personnel receive adequate training on the validation processes.

(U) FBI Response to Recommendation 7: Concur. All Special Agents and Intelligence Analysts receive training on validation during the Basic Field Training Course. Additional training is available, however the FBI will further explore training opportunities for HQ personnel and ensure role and responsivities are better communicated throughout the FBI.

(U)Recommendation 8: OIG recommends FBI re-engineer its process for CHS validation to ensure that the CHSs with the greatest risk factors are selected, that those selections are independently assessed by headquarters, and that continued CHS use determinations receive appropriate headquarters scrutiny.

(U) FBI Response to Recommendation 8: Concur. The FBI has already initiated meetings with D01 to address possible revisions to the AG Guidelines that would better align current FBI resources, personnel, and policies with a cohesive long-term CHS validation strategy. The FBI is assessing other characteristics that might indicate higher risk levels and a need for enhanced scrutiny, as opposed to utilizing long-term continuous handling as the sole criteria for enhanced review. The CHS Policy Guide is in the process of being updated to reflect the most recent changes to the FBI's current validation process, to include the results of the above-mentioned assessment and any resulting changes to the AG Guidelines.

(U)Recommendation 9: OIG recommends FBI ensure that headquarters validation personnel document their analyses, conclusions, and recommendations in validation reports.

(U)FBI Response to Recommendation 9: Concur. FBI will coordinate with the appropriate OGC representatives and DOJ counterparts to discuss validation report content in more detail and how specific findings should be documented.

(U)Recommendation 10: OIG recommends FBI update its Validation Manual to ensure that its annual CHS review process is accurately documented and review and update its annual CHS report to ensure that it sufficiently addresses CHS risks, provide field offices guidance on the updates, and stress to field offices the importance of the annual CHS report in the FBI's validation process.

(U) FBI Response to Recommendation 10: Concur. The DI will update the QSSR and FOASR forms within Delta. The FBI is currently working to update the CHS Validation Manual and fully incorporate it into the CHS Policy Guide, which will incorporate any changes based on the discussions with DOJ on the AG Guidelines.

(U)Recommendation 11: OIG recommends FBI develop and implement a policy that clearly informs FBI personnel of the acceptable platforms for communicating with CHSs and provide training to its workforce on the policy.

(U) **FBI Response to Recommendation 11: Concur.** The FBI has proactively undertaken efforts to address CHS handling and tradecraft matters, with a specific focus on operational communication policy, protocols, and best practices. The FBI has demonstrated a commitment to developing and implementing policy that clearly informs FBI personnel of the acceptable platforms for communicating with CHSs, and to provide training on those platforms to its workforce. All newly adopted policy recommendations and associated prohibitions will be communicated to the workforce in an effort to ensure awareness and compliance.

(U)**Recommendation 12: OIGrecommendsFBIrestrictaccesstothehighlyclassified CHS shared system to only those with a need to know until the system is replaced.**

(U) **FBI Response to Recommendation 12: Concur.** Access to the shared system is restricted to the CHS's handling agent and whoever the handling agent designates as requiring access to their specific CHS's highly classified reporting. No other FBI field office personnel can view the reporting within system. The only individuals at FBI Headquarters that have access to the shared system reporting are the program manager and that program manager's back-up who establishes the shared system folder for the CHS's reporting. The FBI will ensure only those who need to know have access to the system.

(U)**Recommendation 13: OIG recommends FBI take actions to mitigate its gaps in CHS coverage by prioritizing the development of its new threat intelligence and CHS coverage system and ensure that the policies and procedures for its use are documented and accompanied by detailed training on the new system.**

(U) **FBI Response to Recommendation 13: Concur.** The FBI has prioritized the development of a platform that will offer the ability to understand enterprise-wide collection capabilities against FBI threats, and aggregates data to analyze the FBI source posture. The platform will eliminate the need to leverage multiple systems by creating one central location to view this FBI data collection. The platform will be compliant with all FBI policies governing approved datasets coming from FBI Source Systems. Detailed training on use of the platform application will be provided upon its release to the FBI enterprise.

(U)Recommendation 14: OIG recommends FBI consult with all proposed stakeholders that will be responsible for providing data to the new system, identify any other data integrity issues, and document the policies and procedures for ongoing data quality monitoring of its new threat intelligence and CHS coverage system.

(U) FBI Response to Recommendation 14: Concur. The FBI will continue to work with the stakeholders to address data integrity issues related to how the application aggregates federated and ingested data. The FBI has a process in place to track and monitor issues reported pre enterpriserelease. Afterenterprisereleaseuserswillfollowcurrentpracticesofreportingdata integrity and application functionality issues via feedback loops that will be tracked in a SharePoint and or ticketing system.

(U)Recommendation15: OIG recommends the Department and the FBI coordinate to ensure the composition of the HSRC is sufficient and appropriate and includes the requisite skills and knowledge to approve the continued use of FBI's long-term CHSs and seek revisions to the AG Guidelines, as necessary, to memorialize any changes in the composition.

(U) FBI Response to Recommendation 15: Concur. The FBI has already initiated meetings with DOJ to address possible revisions to the AG Guidelines that would better align current FBI resources, personnel and policies with a cohesive long-term CHS validation strategy. This will include discussions of the overall composition of the HSRC and additional methods to ensure the correct personnel with appropriate skills and knowledge are able to attend the committee meetings.

(U) **Recommendation 16: Coordinate to consider establishing additional HSRCs or increasing the frequency of the HSRC meetings until the backlog of CHSs awaiting HSRC approval for continued use is eliminated.**

(U) **FBI Response to Recommendation 16: Concur.** The FBI has already initiated meetings with DOJ to address possible revisions to the AG Guidelines that would better align current FBI resources, personnel, and policies with a cohesive long-term CHS validation strategy. This will include discussions of increasing the frequency of the HSRC and methods to ensure the correct personnel with appropriate skills and knowledge are able to attend the committee meetings.

(U) APPENDIX 4
(U) DEPARTMENT OF JUSTICE'S RESPONSE TO THE DRAFT AUDIT REPORT

U.S. Department of Justice

Office of the Deputy Attorney General

Bradley Weinsheimer
Associate Deputy Attorney General

Washington, D.C. 20530
202-303-7843

MEMORANDUM

TO: Jason R. Malmstrom
Assistant Inspector General
For Audit
Office of the Inspector General

FROM: Bradley Weinsheimer *y. Bradley Weinsheimer*
Associate Deputy Attorney General
Office of the Deputy Attorney General

DATE: September 24, 2019

SUBJECT: Response to OIG's Draft Report: "Audit of the Federal Bureau of Investigation's Management of its Confidential Human Source Validation Process"

The Office of the Deputy Attorney General (ODAG) appreciates the audit undertaken by the Office of the Inspector General (OIG) and the opportunity to comment on OIG's draft audit report, "Audit of the Federal Bureau of Investigation's Management of its Confidential Human Source Validation Process" (the "Report").

The Report sets forth several recommendations. Recommendations One through Fourteen are directed to the Federal Bureau of Investigation (FBI), and I understand the FBI responded separately. We respond below to Recommendations Fifteen and Sixteen, which are directed to both the FBI and the Department.

15. OIG recommends the Department and the FBI coordinate to ensure the composition of the HSRC is sufficient and appropriate and includes the requisite skills and knowledge to approve the continued use of FBI's long-term CHSs and seek revisions to the AG Guidelines, as necessary, to memorialize any changes in the composition.

The Department concurs with this recommendation, and has recently met with the FBI on the composition of the Human Source Review Committee ("HSRC"). The Department and the FBI will ensure the composition of the HSRC is sufficient and appropriate and includes the requisite skills and knowledge to approve the continued use of FBI's long-term CHSs. To the extent necessary, we will seek revisions to the Attorney General's Guidelines in accordance with that determination.

16. Coordinate to consider establishing additional HSRCs or increasing the frequency of the HSRC meetings until the backlog of CHSs awaiting HSRC approval for continued use is eliminated.

The Department concurs with this recommendation, and has recently met with the FBI on the issue of HSRC processing of CHS validations. We will consider establishing additional HSRCs or increasing the frequency of the HSRC meetings until the backlog of CHSs awaiting HSRC approval for continued use is eliminated.

(U) APPENDIX 5
(U) OFFICE OF THE INSPECTOR GENERAL ANALYSIS AND SUMMARY OF ACTIONS NECESSARY TO CLOSE THE REPORT

(U) The OIG provided a draft of this audit report to the Federal Bureau of Investigation (FBI) and the Department of Justice (Department or DOJ). Reponses from the FBI and the Office of the Deputy Attorney General are incorporated in this final report as Appendices 3 and 4, respectfully. In response to our audit report, the FBI and Department concurred with our recommendations and discussed the actions they will implement in response to our findings. As a result, the status of the audit report is resolved. The following provides the OIG analysis of the response and summary of actions necessary to close the report.

(U) **Recommendations for the FBI:**
1. **(U) Ensure that the DI designs, implements, and adheres to validation policies and procedures for its long-term CHSs that comply with the AG Guidelines, or coordinate with the Department to seek revisions to the AG Guidelines, as necessary.**

(U) <u>Resolved.</u> The FBI concurred with our recommendation.

(U) The FBI stated in its response that it has already initiated meetings with the DOJ to address possible revisions to the AG Guidelines that would better align current FBI resources, personnel, and policies with a long-term CHS validation strategy. Additionally, the FBI stated that it is assessing other characteristics that might indicate higher risk levels and a need for enhanced scrutiny, as opposed to utilizing long-term as the sole criteria for enhanced review. Further, the FBI stated that it is in the process of updating its Policy Guide to reflect the most recent changes to the FBI's current validation process, to include the results of the above-mentioned assessment and any revisions to the AG Guidelines.

(U) This recommendation can be closed when the FBI provides evidence that has designed, implemented, and adhered to validation policies or procedures for its long-term CHSs that comply with the AG Guidelines or has coordinated with the Department to seek revisions to the AG Guidelines, as necessary.

2. (U) Dedicate sufficient and appropriately trained personnel to ensure that long-term CHS validations, including backlogged long-term CHS validations, are conducted in accordance with the requirements of the AG Guidelines.

(U) <u>Resolved.</u> The FBI concurred with our recommendation.

(U) The FBI stated in its response that it has initiated meetings with the Department to address possible revisions to the AG Guidelines that would better align current FBI resources, personnel, and policies with a long-term CHS validation strategy. Further, the FBI will evaluate resources and the process to ensure that long-term validations, including any backlog, are conducted in accordance with the requirements of the AG Guidelines.

(U) This recommendation can be closed when the FBI provides evidence that it has dedicated sufficient and appropriately trained personnel to ensure that long-term CHS validations, including backlogged long-term CHS validations, are conducted in accordance with the requirements of the AG Guidelines.

3. (U) Coordinate with the Department and update, as necessary, its long-term CHS validation report to ensure that it addresses the appropriate scope of review and memorializes any validation personnel's conclusions or recommendations.

(U) <u>Resolved.</u> The FBI concurred with our recommendation.

(U) The FBI stated in its response that it has initiated meetings with the Department to address possible revisions to the AG Guidelines that would better align current FBI resources, personnel, and policies with a long-term CHS validation strategy. Additionally, the FBI stated that this may result in a new validation product with a new set of parameters for period of review, depth of analysis, and responsible personnel. Further, the FBI stated that the inclusion of recommendations and conclusions in the validation report will be discussed with the Department and the FBI's Office of General Counsel (OGC).

(U) This recommendation can be closed when the FBI provides evidence that it has coordinated with the Department and updated, as necessary, its long term CHS validation report to ensure that it addresses the appropriate scope of review and memorializes any validation personnel's conclusions or recommendations.

4. (U) Develop and implement an automated mechanism in its Delta system to ensure that long-term CHSs are accurately identified and monitored, including an automated notification to the headquarters unit responsible for conducting long-term CHS validations.

(U) <u>Resolved.</u> The FBI concurred with our recommendation.

(U) The FBI stated in its response that it deployed an automated mechanism in its Delta system to ensure long-term CHSs are accurately identified and monitored, including a notification to headquarters, in August 2019. Further, the FBI stated that the automated mechanism is currently being tested to ensure accuracy.

(U) This recommendation can be closed when the FBI provides evidence it has developed and implemented an automated mechanism in its Delta system to ensure that long-term CHSs are accurately identified and monitored, including an automated notification to the headquarters unit responsible for conducting long-term CHS validations.

5. (U) Develop and implement an automated workflow in Delta to ensure that all handling agents request and document SAC approval or disapproval for the continued handling of CHSs in excess of 5 years.

(U) <u>Resolved.</u> The FBI concurred with our recommendation.

(U) The FBI stated in its response that it is currently working on automating SAC approval or disapproval for continued handling of a CHS in excess of 5 years and deployment of this process is tentatively scheduled for second quarter of FY 2020.

(U) This recommendation can be closed when the FBI provides evidence that it has developed and implemented an automated workflow in Delta to ensure that all handling agents request and document SAC approval or disapproval for the continued handling of CHSs in excess of 5 years.

6. (U) Update its Policy Guide to formally incorporate its Validation Manual in accordance with the IPO Policy Directive to ensure current validation processes and procedures are in compliance with AG Guidelines requirements.

(U) <u>Resolved.</u> The FBI concurred with our recommendation.

(U) The FBI stated in its response that it is working to update its Validation Manual and fully incorporate it into its Policy Guide. Further, the FBI stated that the Policy Guide will ensure compliance with the AG Guidelines.

(U) This recommendation can be closed when the FBI provides evidence that it has updated its Policy Guide to formally incorporate its Validation Manual in accordance with the IPO Policy Directive to ensure current validation processes and procedures are in compliance with AG Guidelines requirements.

7. **(U) Ensure all validation process roles and responsibilities are defined and field office personnel receive adequate training on the validation processes.**

(U) <u>Resolved.</u> The FBI concurred with our recommendation.

(U) The FBI stated in its response that it provides all Special Agents and Intelligence Analysts with validation training during its Basic Field Training Course. While the OIG acknowledges that validation training is provided during its Basic Field Training Course, the OIG found that the FBI's guidance and messaging related to its newest validation process for CHSs with characteristics the FBI believed were significant was inadequate. As noted in our report, the guidance included subjective criteria for which CHSs should be forwarded to headquarters and provided no documentation that certain field office personnel had received guidance on their roles and responsibilities related to the new validation process. Further, in December 2018, the FBI's Resource Planning Office found that, historically, changes to validation processes have not been effectively communicated to field offices.

(U) This recommendation can be closed when the FBI provides evidence that all validation process roles and responsibilities are defined and field office personnel receive adequate training on the validation processes.

8. **(U) Reengineer its process for CHS validation to ensure that the CHSs with the greatest risk factors are selected, that those selections are independently assessed by headquarters, and that continued CHS use determinations receive appropriate headquarters scrutiny.**

(U) <u>Resolved.</u> The FBI concurred with our recommendation.

(U) The FBI stated in its response that it has initiated meetings with the Department to address possible revisions to the AG Guidelines that would better align current FBI resources, personnel, and policies with a long-term CHS validation strategy. In addition, the FBI stated that it is assessing other characteristics that may indicate higher risk levels and a need for enhanced scrutiny. Further, the FBI stated that it is in the process of updating its Policy Guide to reflect the results of the above-mentioned assessment and any resulting changes to the AG Guidelines.

(U) This recommendation can be closed when the FBI provides evidence that it has reengineered its process for CHS validation to ensure that the CHSs with the greatest risk factors are selected, that those selections are independently assessed by headquarters, and that continued CHS use determinations receive appropriate headquarters scrutiny.

9. (U) Ensure that headquarters validation personnel document their analyses, conclusions, and recommendations in validation reports.

(U) <u>Resolved.</u> The FBI concurred with our recommendation.

(U) The FBI stated in its response that it will coordinate with appropriate OGC representatives and DOJ counterparts to discuss validation report content in more detail and how specific findings should be documented.

(U) This recommendation can be closed when the FBI provides evidence that ensures that headquarters validation personnel document their analyses, conclusions, and recommendations in validation reports.

10. (U) Update its Validation Manual to ensure that its annual CHS review process is accurately documented and review and update its annual CHS report to ensure that it sufficiently addresses CHS risks, provide field offices guidance on the updates, and stress to field offices the important of the annual CHS report in the FBI's validation process.

(U) <u>Resolved.</u> The FBI concurred with our recommendation.

(U) The FBI stated in its response that it the DI will updated its quarterly and annualCHSreportformswithinDelta. Further,- theFBIstatedthatitis currently working to update its Validation Manual and fully incorporate it into its Policy Guide, which will incorporate any changes based on the discussion with DOJ on the AG Guidelines.

(U) This recommendation can be closed when the FBI provides evidence it has updated its Validation Manual to ensure that its annual CHS review process is accurately documented and review and update its annual CHS report to ensure that it sufficiently addresses CHS risks, provide field offices guidance on the updates, and stress to field offices the important of the annual CHS report in the FBI's validation process.

11. (U) Develop and implement a policy that clearly informs FBI personnel of the acceptable platforms for communicating with CHSs and provide training to its workforce on the policy.

(U) <u>Resolved.</u> The FBI concurred with our recommendation.

(U) The FBI stated in its response that it has undertaken efforts to address CHS matters, including a specific focus on operational communication policy, protocols, and best practices. The FBI also stated that it has demonstrated a commitment to developing and implementing policy that clearly provides information to FBI personnel regarding acceptable platforms for communicating with CHSs and providing training on those platforms. However, as noted in our report, the OIG found varying uses of communication platforms among FBI handing agents due to a lack of clear guidance for CHS communications.

(U) This recommendation can be closed when the FBI provides evidence that it has developed and implemented a policy that clearly informs FBI personnel of the acceptable platforms for com-

---

municating with CHSs and provide training to its workforce on the policy.

12. (U) Restrict access to its highly classified CHS shared system to only those with a need to know until the system is replaced.

(U) <u>Resolved.</u> The FBI concurred with our recommendation.

(U//FOUO) The FBI stated in its response that access to the shared system is restricted to the CHS's handling agent and whoever the handling agent designates as requiring access to their specific CHS's highly classified reporting and that no other FBI field office personnel can view the reporting within the system. Further, the FBI stated that the only individuals at FBI headquarters that have access to the shared system are the program manager and that program manager's backup. However, as noted in our report the OIG learned that the shared system was not properly secured [REDACTED] did not possess the requisite "need to know." The FBI stated in its response that it will ensure that only those who need to know will have access to the system.

(U) This recommendation can be closed when the FBI provides evidence that it has restricted access to its CHS shared system to only those with a need to know until the system is replaced.

13. (U) Take actions to mitigate its gaps in CHS coverage by prioritizing the development of its new threat intelligence and CHS coverage system and ensure that the policies and procedures for its use are documented and accompanied by detailed training on the new system.

(U) <u>Resolved.</u> The FBI concurred with our recommendation.

(U) The FBI stated in its response that it has prioritized the development of a platform that will offer the ability to understand enterprise-wide collection capabilities against FBI threats, and aggregates data to analyze FBI CHS posture. Inaddition,theFBI-statedthattheplatformwilleliminatetheneed to leverage multiple systems by creating one central location to view this FBI data collection. Further, the FBI stated that the platform will be compliant with all FBI policies governing approved datasets from FBI systems and detailed training on the system will be provided upon its release to the FBI enterprise.

(U) This recommendation can be closed when the FBI provides evidence it has taken actions to mitigate its gaps in CHS coverage by prioritizing the development of its new threat intelligence and CHS coverage system and ensure that the policies and procedures for its use are documented and accompanied by detailed training on the new system.

14. (U) Consult with all proposed stakeholders that will be responsible for providing data to the new system, identify any other data integrity issues, and document the policies and procedures for ongoing data quality monitoring of its new threat intelligence and CHS coverage system.

(U) Resolved. The FBI concurred with our recommendation.

(U) The FBI stated in its response that it will continue to work with stakeholder to address data integrity issues related to how the proposed threat intelligence and CHS coverage system aggregates federated and ingesteddata. Inaddition,theFBIstatedthatithasaprocessinplaceto track and monitor issues reported pre-enterprise release. Lastly, it stated that after enterprise release, users of the system will follow current practices of reporting data integrity and application functionality issues via feedback loops that will be tracked.

(U) This recommendation can be closed when the FBI provides evidence that it has consulted with all proposed stakeholders that will be responsible for providing data to the new system, identify any other data integrity issues, and document the policies and procedures for ongoing data quality monitoring of its new threat intelligence and CHS coverage system.

(U) Recommendations for the Department and the FBI:

15. (U) Coordinate to ensure the composition of the HSRC is sufficient and appropriate and includes the requisite skills and knowledge to approve the continued use of FBI's long-term CHSs and seek revisions to the AG Guidelines, as necessary, to memorialize any changes in the composition.

(U) <u>Resolved.</u> The Department and the FBI concurred with our recommendation.

(U) The Department stated in its response that it has recently met with the FBI on the composition of the HSRC and that the Department and the FBI will ensure the composition of the HSRC is sufficient and appropriate and includes the requisite skills and knowledge to approve the continued use of FBI's long termCHSs. Further,theDepartmentstatedthat,totheextentnecessary,it will seek revisions to the AG Guidelines.

(U) The FBI stated in its response it has already initiated meetings with the Department to address possible revisions to the AG Guidelines that would better align current FBI resources, personnel, and policies with a cohesive long-term CHS validation strategy. This will include discussions of the overall composition of the HSRC and additional methods to ensure the correct personnel with appropriate skills and knowledge are able to attend the committee meetings.

(U) This recommendation can be closed when the Department and the FBI provide evidence that it has coordinated to ensure the composition of the HSRC is sufficient and appropriate and includes the requisite skills and knowledge to approve the continued use of FBI's long-term CHSs and seek revisions to the AG Guidelines, as necessary, to memorialize any changes in the composition.

16. (U) Coordinate to consider establishing additional HSRCs or increasing the frequency of the HSRC meetings until the backlog of CHSs awaiting HSRC approval for continued use is eliminated.

(U) <u>Resolved.</u> The Department and the FBI concurred with our recommendation.

(U) The Department stated in its response that it has recently met with the FBI on the issue of HSRC processing of validations and that it will consider
establishing additional HSRCs or increasing the frequency of the HSRC meetings until the backlog of CHSs awaiting HSRC approval for continued use is eliminated.

(U) The FBI stated in its response that it has already initiated meetings with the Department to address possible revisions to the AG Guidelines that would better align current FBI resources, personnel, and policies with a cohesive long-term CHS validation strategy. The FBI further stated that this will include discussions of increasing the frequency of the HSRC and methods to ensure the correct personnel with appropriate skills and knowledge are able to attend the committee meetings.

(U) This recommendation can be closed when the Department and the FBI provide evidence that it has coordinated to consider establishing additional HSRCs or increasing the frequency of the HSRC meetings until the backlog of CHSs awaiting HSRC approval for continued use is eliminated.

The Department of Justice Office of the Inspector General (DOJ OIG) is a statutorily created independent entity whose mission is to detect and deter waste, fraud, abuse, and misconduct in the Department of Justice, and to promote economy and efficiency in the Department's operations.

To report allegations of waste, fraud, abuse, or misconduct regarding DOJ programs, employees, contractors, grants, or contracts please visit or call the DOJ OIG Hotline at oig.justice.gov/hotline or (800) 869-4499.

U.S. DEPARTMENT OF JUSTICE OFFICE OF THE INSPECTOR GENERAL

950 Pennsylvania Avenue, NW
Washington, DC 20530-0001

Website: oig.justice.gov
Twitter: @JusticeOIG
YouTube: JusticeOIG
Also at Oversight.gov

OTHER BOOKS BY SASTRUGI PRESS

2024 Total Eclipse State Series by Aaron Linsdau

Sastrugi Press has published state-specific and country guides for the 2024 total eclipse crossing over North America. Check the Sastrugi Press website for the available eclipse books for Texas, Arkansas, Oklahoma, Missouri, Kentucky, Illinois, Indiana, Ohio, Pennsylvania, New York, Vermont, New Hampshire, Maine, Mexico, and Canada.

www.sastrugipress.com/eclipse

50 Wildlife Hotspots by Moose Henderson

Find out where to find animals and photograph them in Grand Teton National Park from a professional wildlife photographer. This unique guide shares the secret locations with the best chance at spotting wildlife.

A Small Pile of Feathers by Gerry Spence

Gerry Spence reveals his spiritual, loving, and sometimes humorous sides, depicted in his devotion to family and to preserving the wild places he writes of as though they were inscribed on his own bones and in his own blood.

Adventure Expedition One by Aaron Linsdau and Terry Williams M.D.

How do you set off on your first epic expedition? Where should you even start? This book has practical advice to help you begin planning your first trek. Dreaming, planning, training, doing, and returning alive are all covered in this guide.

Alaska: Illustrated Guide for the Curious by Nikki Mann and Jeff Wohl

This friendly, illustrated field guide presents interesting and educational information on Alaska's most common land and marine creatures and their habitats. With this book you can learn bear safety, edible berries, tracking, how glaciers are shaping Alaska, the creatures in a tidepool, and so much more. Curious explorers of all ages will enjoy referencing this vibrant guide as you explore the wonder of Alaska.

Along the Sylvan Trail by Julianne Couch

Along the Sylvan Trail dips into the lives of linked characters as they confront futures that aren't clearly dictated by conventional planning. The conflicts of the small town change and pressure residents of Sylvan Grove to look beyond their world to the outside.

Antarctic Tears by Aaron Linsdau

What would make someone give up a high-paying career to ski alone across Antarctica to the South Pole? This inspirational true story will make readers both cheer and cry. Fighting skin-freezing temperatures, infections, and emotional breakdown,

Aaron Linsdau exposes the harsh realities of the world's largest wilderness. Discover what drives someone to the brink of destruction to pursue a dream.

Cache Creek by Susan Marsh

Five minutes from the hubbub of Jackson's town square, Cache Creek offers the chance for hikers to immerse themselves in wild nature. It is a popular hiking, biking, and cross-country ski area on the outskirts of Jackson Hole, Wyoming.

Cloudshade by Lori Howe, Ph.D.

The poems of Cloudshade breathe with the vivid, fragrant essence of life in every season on America's high plains. Extraordinarily relatable, the poems of Cloudshade swing wide a door to life in the West, both for lovers of poetry and for those who don't normally read poems.

The Diary of a Dude Wrangler by Struthers Burt

The dude ranch world of Struthers Burt was a romantic destination in the early twentieth century. They transported people back to the Wild West. These ranches were and still are popular destinations. Experience the old west through this dude rancher's writing.

Journeys to the Edge by Randall Peeters, Ph.D.

What is it like to climb Mount Everest? Is it possible for you to actually make the ascent? It requires dreaming big and creating a personal vision to climb the mountains in your life. Randall Peeters shares his successes and failures and gives you some directly applicable guidelines on how you can create a vision for your life.

Lost at Windy Corner by Aaron Linsdau

Windy Corner on Denali has claimed lives, fingers, and toes. What would make someone brave lethal weather, crevasses, and slick ice to attempt to summit North America's highest mountain? The author shares the lessons Denali teaches on managing goals and risks. Apply the message to build resilience and overcome adversity.

Prevailing Westerlies by Ed Lavino

With clarity and intensity, Lavino's photographs express a longing for the natural world and hope for its future. An intimacy with the Rocky Mountain West born of long familiarity and close observation is evident. These beautiful black and white images are timeless, yet decidedly modern.

Roaming the Wild by Grover Ratliff

Experience the landscape and wildlife photography of Grover Ratliff in this unique volume. Jackson Hole is home to some of the most iconic landscapes in North America. In this land of harsh winters and short summers, wildlife survives and thrives. People from all around the world travel here to savor the rare vistas.

Sagebrush Alley by Patricia Jones

What's worse than having a stalker? Being pursued by a second one who has already killed. Attempting to complete her studies, Dana Cameron has to avoid becoming a murder victim. She becomes tangled in a struggle for life trapped in a claustrophobic nightmare.

Sleeping Dogs Don't Lie by Michael McCoy

A young Native American boy is taken from his home after tragedy strikes, grows up in middle America, and through his first real adult summer searches for Wyoming artifacts, falls in with the subversive Dog Soldiers Resurrected, and attempts single-handedly to solve the mystery behind the murder of his treasured coworker.

So I Said by Gerry Spence

The collected sayings of Gerry Spence prods readers into thinking about their own vision of the world. As a lawyer with decades of experience in defending the defenseless, he's fought against giants. His insights provide a grander vision of how the nearly invisible world of the justice system in So I Said.

The Burqa Cave by Dean Petersen

Still haunted by Iraq, Tim Ross finds solace teaching high school in Wyoming. That is, until freshman David Jenkins reveals the murder of a lost local girl. Will Tim be able to overcome his demons to stop the murderer?

The Mueller Report by Robert Mueller

The U.S. Justice Department assigned Robert Mueller and a team of agents in the spring of 2017 to investigate accusations of collusion between President Donald Trump and Russian operatives. This is the complete text of the declassified, redacted report. Available in paperback, hardback, large-print, and ebook.

Voices at Twilight by Lori Howe, Ph.D.

Voices at Twilight is a guide that takes readers on a visual tour of twelve past and present Wyoming ghost towns. Contained within are travel directions, GPS coordinates, and tips for intrepid readers.www.sastrugipress.com

Do you enjoy classic literature? Sastrugi Press has a classic series just for you. Visit our webpage and find more quality books like this one at www.sastrugipress.com/classics/.

Visit Sastrugi Press on the web at www.sastrugipress.com to purchase the above titles in bulk. They are also available from your local bookstore or online retailers in print, e-book, or audiobook form. Thank you for choosing Sastrugi Press.